THE PRESENT

ANDREA TORREY BALSARA

THE PRESENT

ANDREA TORREY BALSARA

www.pearsoned.co.nz

Your comments on this title are welcome at
feedback@pearsoned.co.nz

Pearson
a division of Pearson New Zealand Ltd
67 Apollo Drive, Rosedale, Auckland 0632, New Zealand

Associated companies throughout the world

The Present

Story by Andrea Torrey Balsara

U.S. edition by Houghton Mifflin Harcourt Publishing Company

All rights reserved. No part of this work may be reproduced or
transmitted in any form or by any means, electronic or mechanical,
including photocopying or recording, or by any information storage and
retrieval system, without the prior written permission of the copyright
owner unless such copying is expressly permitted by federal copyright
law. Requests for permission to make copies of any part of the work
should be addressed to Houghton Mifflin Harcourt Publishing Company,
Attn: Contracts, Copyrights, and Licensing, 9400 Southpark Center
Loop, Orlando, Florida 32819.

Printed in China via Pearson Education Asia (EPC/01)

ISBN 978-0-5479-8623-4

10 9 8 7 6   1846   12 11 10
4500000000   A B C D E F G

If you have received these materials as examination copies free of
charge, Houghton Mifflin Harcourt Publishing Company retains title
to the materials and they may not be resold. Resale of examination
copies is strictly prohibited.

Possession of this publication in print format does not entitle users to
convert this publication, or any portion of it, into electronic format.

AUTHOR NOTE

A couple of years ago I heard someone refer to "the emotional abandonment of children" and it got me thinking. When I think of an abandoned child, images of gaunt street children come to mind. Emotional abandonment was something I had never thought of before: parents too busy with their careers, or single parents working day and night to keep food on the table; parents so overwhelmed with their own emotional lives that they have nothing left to give, even to their child.

Originally, when I began to write *The Present*, I thought the theme would be emotional abandonment, and it is. But the story evolved into something else as well. It also became a story about being human: making horrible mistakes and finding forgiveness and love.

Andrea Torrey Balsara

CHAPTER ONE

Rudy is a ridiculous name for a dog, but that's the name of the dog that my dad gave to me for my fourteenth birthday—a weird boxer-golden retriever mix with a mashed face and a furry tail. It was the last week in June, summer vacation was in full swing, and my friends were in my backyard for my birthday party. We were playing water volleyball in the pool when my mom walked over, wearing an enormous smile on her face and holding a frilly looking present. She said, "Julie, it's time to open presents," like I was four, not fourteen.

"It's okay, Mom, I'll open them later," I said. "We're just hanging out for now." The smile on Mom's face completely vanished, and then my friends started hauling themselves out of the pool—many of them have seen Mom become irritated before. Suddenly, there was this crash, and a loud *WOOF!*

Jessica Striker shrieked, "It's a DOG!" (Dogs scare her because one bit her when she was five or something, and she still has the scar on her cheek.) This alien-looking mutt was barreling into the backyard, and attached to the end of its leash was my helpless father. The dog was straining so hard that its tongue was purple and its eyes bulged. Dad's did, too, as he tried desperately to control the lunging, rampaging beast.

"Charlie, what is that?" Mom asked, standing there, holding that present, with a look on her face like she noticed something decomposing. Dad hauled the dog over, pressed the leash into my dumfounded hands, and collapsed into a deckchair.

"His name is Rudy, and he's all yours—happy birthday, baby!" He rubbed his hand over his face and sighed.

My mom gasped—at first she was speechless—but then her voice came back thundering. "Have you completely lost your mind? Don't you think I might want a little prior notice about getting a dog, especially such a hideous, slobbery—"

"It's okay, Mom. I adore him," I said, interrupting.

"Julie, this is between your father and me," she snapped.

"Come on, Claire," said my dad. "I know he's not a pedigreed show dog, but this guy at the office was going to put him to sleep, and I was thinking about how much Julie has wanted a dog, so I claimed him."

"*This* present was from us!" she exclaimed, shaking the forlorn-looking present in front of his face. "*Remember?*" Why did I even bother getting something? You always do this to me."

"How can I always do this to you when I've never brought home a dog before? I try to do something nice—you know what—forget it, I'm leaving!" Dad jerked himself out of the deckchair and stomped back around the house, my mom angrily trailing after him.

"You come back here!" she yelled. "I won't let you ruin Julie's party!" She was still shouting when my dad's engine roared to life. Then the tires squealed, and after that there was awkward silence.

My friends stared, wide-eyed, like they were experiencing a horror movie first-hand: Megan, her boyfriend Kevin, Jessica, Samantha, Suze, and Brianna. My ears pounded as if the entire ocean was in my head, crashing against my skull, and threatening to drown my brain in embarrassment. I rolled my eyes and attempted a laugh, but it sounded more like a cough. I said, "It's so hard to raise parents these days." That sounded lame, even to me, and nobody bothered to laugh, even politely.

Then Megan said, "Last one in the pool's a rotten egg," and that broke the spell. Everyone kind of shook the awkwardness off, and the pounding slowly fell away. I'd forgotten about Rudy, so of course he lunged and ripped his leash out of my hand before sailing into the pool, doing a perfect belly flop.

I think Rudy's a smart dog—I borrowed a training video from the library and have taught him a few basic commands. I can hold out my hand and say, "Stay," and he does. If I want him to come, I just slap my hand on my chest and say in a loud, commanding voice, "COME." It's pretty cool.

Two days after my party, my dad left my mom, and I guess I wasn't surprised, but I was still surprised—do you know what I mean? It's like when you feel something terrible is coming, but when it does you're shocked and thinking, *Wow, I can't believe it!* It took my mom by surprise, too. I remember sitting on the grass in the backyard and hearing their final argument.

"Who is she?"

"Why does there have to be anybody else when you're so—"

"When I'm so *what?* And what about you? You are so—"

Clouds drifted lazily across the sky, and even though it was not yet 11:00 in the morning, it was already becoming uncomfortably warm. A cicada buzzed on a nearby sycamore tree—it sounded like a drill boring holes in the thick air.

"Her name is Evie! There, are you happy?"

"I knew it!"

Rudy put his enormous, heavy head on my leg, his coarse fur prickling my bare skin, but I didn't mind. I scratched behind his ears, and he groaned and drooled on my leg. When I stared into the sky, I swear one of the clouds passing above us was shaped like a dog with a mashed face.

The moving van pulled up, brakes squealing as it shuddered to a stop in front of the house. I watched from behind the curtain of my bedroom window as Dad emerged from the truck with one of his friends and walked over to a pile of things in the middle of our lawn.

"That woman never lets up, does she?" Dad said, shaking his head. He kicked a baseball mitt lying on top of the stack, and it flew off and slapped against the house near my window. THUNK! I stepped back from the window hurriedly and nearly fell over Rudy, who sat by my side, panting, while his slobber dripped on the carpet.

"Julie, come here—I need help carrying out your father's junk!" My mom's voice was shrill, and I ignored her until the door suddenly swung open, and Mom stood there, seething. I could see her lips moving, but, honestly, I couldn't hear anything because the ocean in my head had returned; however, I could see she was mad. She was holding a pile of my dad's T-shirts in front of her, shaking them, and I understood that she wanted me to take them, but my arms felt so heavy.

"Here, take them!" Her shouts finally reached me, and my arms reluctantly stretched out, looking like naked branches on a tree. Suddenly, Rudy jumped up and thundered by Mom, almost knocking her off her feet and causing T-shirts to cascade like falling leaves onto the floor.

"Hey, you . . ." Mom said, turning, but Rudy was already gone. I looked through the window and saw Rudy in the front yard, galloping back and forth as my dad and his friend loaded stuff into the moving van, as if it were a game. Too late, I saw Rudy sniffing around a pile of underwear and socks before lifting his leg.

"Stupid dog!" bellowed my dad, red-faced, as he threw a CD at Rudy. The CD case caught Rudy on the haunch, which then caused him to yelp and run. When my mom erupted in high-pitched laughter, I turned away from the window and saw her nearly doubled-over.

"Good boy!" Mom said, gurgling. At least she and Rudy were finally bonding.

Eventually Dad left, and the curious neighbors, rubberneckers, and people-who-were-shocked eventually got bored and went inside their houses. It was just me, my mom, Rudy, and a big, empty house. Actually, it wasn't empty—it was a mess from a jumble of things: socks, underwear, shirts, scattered car magazines, various books (my dad's), and plant dirt where Mom had tossed out plants Dad had given her. The house just *felt* empty.

There was a smell in the air: roasting chicken. Someone next door must be having roast chicken, and I imagined someone cooking it, maybe making a salad, and pouring milk or juice for drinks before calling the rest of the family to sit and eat. Rudy lifted his nose in the air and sniffed before looking at me. When he did, I swear his eyes were full of tears.

CHAPTER TWO

I can't remember the first day after my dad left, which you might have difficulty believing, but it's true. However, I must have eaten something, and I must have slept, too, because I wasn't starving or sleep-deprived when I finally did notice time passing. I don't know if my dad phoned or if any of my friends phoned, either. Mom wasn't in the mood to take messages, if you know what I mean. I hope they did, though. After I snapped out of my daze, I called my dad's cell phone, but there was no answer. I tried to phone Megan, too, but her mom said she was out with Kevin and asked if she could give me a call when she came back. There was no noise from my mom's room, although there were empty Chinese take-out cartons on the coffee table, so I knew she was probably around somewhere.

I decided to take Rudy out, and we went along the river where thin strands of river grass were combed over the mud after the river had overflowed its banks. That's where we walked, our feet sinking into the sandy mud, Rudy's paw print making almost as big a hole as my foot. Old coffee cups and plastic bags clung against the reeds higher up the bank. Rudy sniffed every blade of river grass and reed, and if they really smelled good, he chewed it daintily.

As we walked back down our street, I thought about how nice it was, so I decided to stop and visit Jessica, who lives three houses down from me. I rang the bell, and her dad answered the door. Mr. Striker is a math teacher at my school, and he's nice, I guess, but he speaks so slowly. I actually do a very funny imitation of him that cracks Megan up, but I don't do it around Jessica: "Uh . . . class . . . uh . . . open your books to . . . uh . . . page three . . . uh . . ."

"Hi, Mr. Striker," I said. "Is Jessica home?"

"Hello, Julie. Uh . . . no, she's out with her . . . mom." He stepped out onto the porch and lowered his head toward me, as if he was going to tell me something top secret. "Uh . . . Julie," he said in a low voice, "I heard about your family's . . . uh . . . troubles."

"Oh yeah?" I said nervously, taking a step back and crunching Rudy's paw. "Sorry, Rudy," I said as he yelped loudly and gave me an indignant look.

"Rudy, eh?" Mr. Striker asked with a smile, leaning over to scratch Rudy behind the ears. "Hello, Rudy. Nice to . . . uh . . . meet you." He kept scratching as Rudy groaned and leaned against Mr. Striker's leg, and Mr. Striker looked back up at me, his forehead creasing into rows of concerned wrinkles. "Julie, I . . . uh . . . want you to know how . . . uh . . . sorry we all are."

He stopped scratching Rudy and looked straight into my eyes. His eyes were blue with tiny flecks of gold—I'd never noticed that before. I couldn't say anything; my tongue felt thick lying in my mouth as if it was a log or a stone or something, so I just nodded and shrugged.

His eyes looked so sad, so I nodded again and tried to smile, but the edges of my mouth began to shake with the effort. Luckily, Rudy immediately collapsed on the welcome mat and rolled onto his back when Mr. Striker had stopped petting him, so I don't think Mr. Striker noticed me. He knelt and scratched Rudy's belly until the dog moaned with pleasure, his eyes half-closed. Then Mr. Striker looked up at me and smiled. "You're . . . uh . . .

a good kid, Julie. I know that . . . uh . . . things will turn out . . . uh . . . okay for you." I suddenly never wanted to show anyone my impression of Mr. Striker again.

I don't know why I cried walking home, but for once Rudy didn't strain at the leash, which was a good thing. When I opened the door to the house, there was no sign of Mom and no new take-out containers, either, so I knocked on her bedroom door.

"Mom?" I asked. There was a rustling sound. "Mom, are you in there?" There was no answer, so I poked my head into her room and saw her lying crossway, face up, over the king-size bed, and still in her pajamas. She was asleep but had makeup stains running down her cheeks and a snot bubble that went in and out with her soft snores. I wiped her nose (and got a little snot on me, which was gross, but I washed my hands afterward) and tucked the quilt over her before creeping out and shutting the door behind me.

"Come on, Rudy," I whispered. "I'll make you a feast."

I made myself some peanut butter toast and a few pieces for Rudy, too. It's actually one of my favorite things to eat, so that was fine, and Rudy gulped it down and then sat smacking his lips, trying to get the peanut butter to go down. The sun was setting, shining through the sliding doors in the kitchen, so Rudy and I sat on the couch in the living room with the lights out. Sometimes I like it better that way because it's more relaxing, you know? I could hear the clock ticking on the wall, and for whatever reason it made me get the phone and dial Megan's number.

"Is that Julie?" asks Mrs. Bartlet when I ask for Megan. "She's not here, honey—she had to go out again, but she told me she'll try to phone you later, okay? Are you going to be at home, dear?"

I looked around the living room and shrugged, not that Mrs. Bartlett could see. "Yeah, I guess. Thanks."

"That's okay, honey. And Julie?"

Oh no. "Yes, Mrs. Bartlet?"

"I'm sorry about your mom and dad, honey—really sorry."

"Thanks . . . Bye."

That stupid clock was really getting on my nerves, so I turned on the TV to drown it out, but nothing good was on. There was a boring dance contest with famous people, some kind of debate with really boring people, and a boring movie that I'd already seen and didn't feel like watching again. I flipped the channels so much that Rudy looked up at me and whined, but I didn't blame him; it would have bugged me, too, if someone else had been doing it. He kept staring at me, so I turned the TV off, and he laid his head down, smacking his lips. I picked up the phone and tried to call my dad again. I thought, you know, maybe he had finished moving in and now he could answer the phone, but it rang and rang, and no one picked it up.

I am standing on top of a mountain, and the view is amazing. I can breathe here; I fill my lungs and smell clean snow, wild meadow flowers, and fresh air. There are mountains everywhere, and the sky is so blue. I make the mistake of looking down and see an ocean far below with thick, black water. Suddenly, the ocean starts to whirl, like ink

going down a drain. I try to stay still, but where I'm standing becomes loose rock. My feet scramble, but the stones roll out from under me, and my legs fail. I fall toward the swirling ink, and there is a ringing in my ears as the ocean rushes to meet me . . . a ringing . . .

———

"Finally!" Megan exclaimed when I answer the phone. "Did you go out or something?"

"No, I was here," I said, holding the phone to my ear. "I was just—I must have fallen asleep."

"That's cool," she said, giggling. "I just got back from my date. Do you want to hear about it?"

"Maybe tomorrow, okay? I'm feeling kind of . . . you know."

"Oh, yeah," she said. "How are you? I'm sorry I haven't phoned, but I thought you might want some space; I know I would if I were you."

"Yeah, thanks. I'm . . . um . . ." I tried to focus. "I'm okay—just hanging out."

"Okay. Do you want to come over tomorrow? Kevin is helping his dad with some stupid thing at work, so I'm not doing anything, and my mom said you could bring your dog. What's his name again?"

"Rudy," I said. "Yeah, that'd be great. I'll get there somehow—maybe I'll ride my bike." Mom usually drove me, but I really wanted to see Megan, and I didn't think Mom would be in the mood to drive me anywhere right then. After I hung up, I brushed my teeth and got into my pajamas. I went to get into bed, but Rudy had got there first and was sprawled across it, blinking up at me, all innocent. I pushed him, and he snorted at me but finally moved over. I slept with my back against his and didn't have any more dreams that I could remember.

CHAPTER THREE

When I got up the next morning, Mom was gone and so was her car; she had probably she'd gone to work or something. She's the manager at a bank.

The dishes in the sink were starting to smell, so I did them, and then I wiped down the table and swept the kitchen floor. I had to—everywhere I stepped, crumbs or something crunched under my feet, and I really hate that. Finished cleaning, I poured out some cereal for myself while Rudy stared at me with a you-never-feed-me look. "Yeah, yeah, you can wait," I said. I took the milk out of the refrigerator, but when I poured some on my cereal, I swear it came out in chunks.

"Gee, you think it's bad or something, Rudy? What do you say to peanut butter toast again?" He panted at me, and it looked like he was smiling, so I guess that meant yes. I dumped the cereal and made us both some toast.

Rudy was still smacking his lips when we finally got going to Megan's. I had to pump up my tires and make a leash from a long piece of rope so Rudy could run next to me. Of course, the first thing he did was to lunge in front of the bike, but then he sort of got the hang of it. We rode for about ten minutes, and I saw all sorts of things I normally didn't notice because I never usually rode that far.

I was staring at an old graveyard on top of a big hill when I drove my bike into a ditch. Rudy landed on top of me, knocking the wind right out of me, and we both sat there for a minute, just breathing and determining if anything was broken.

"Heel, Rudy!" I called, trying to stay upright on my bike as Rudy raced up the side of the ditch, pulling me behind him. Despite three close calls, we made it out of the ditch—still, I reminded myself to teach Rudy what "heel" meant.

When we finally got to Megan's, I tried to stop, but Rudy kept going, and we kind of crashed into the garage door. Luckily, it didn't hurt too much, and Rudy stood there panting at me with a smile on his face.

"Oh ha, ha, ha," I said.

Mrs. Bartlet answered when I knocked. She was like one of those mothers you see in the movies, you know what I mean? Her cheeks looked like two red apples, and her short dark hair was a mass of soft curls. She was wearing an apron and was just taking off oven mitts. A buttery, baking smell wafted out the door.

"Julie, come in! It's so good to see you, dear." She held open the door. "Megan's on the phone, but did you want to try some of my cookies? Come and sit down and I'll get you a plate." She bustled off.

I hesitated because I didn't know what to do with Rudy. She must have felt it through the walls or something, because she called from the kitchen. "And, honey, don't be shy about bringing in your dog. This house has seen worse, believe me!" So we both walked right in. Rudy sank onto the carpet and fell asleep instantly. The run must have really worn him out if he could sleep through the smell of those cookies; however, I drank milk and crunched sugar cookies—I don't know how many. She kept bringing them, so I figured she must have enough. After I had eaten maybe a hundred, Megan finally came out of her room and hugged me.

"I've missed you, Jules," she said.

We sat on Megan's bed while Rudy was snored loudly beside it. He'd dragged himself to Megan's room when we went in there and immediately dropped into a coma again.

"So how's it been?" she asked, leaning with her back against the wall, making a thick ponytail of her long black hair that always looks good, even smashed against the wall.

I shrugged and stared up at the ceiling. "Did you know you've got a crack that goes all the way along the wall?"

Megan shrugged, too. "Who cares?" She put an elastic band on her ponytail and tossed it over her shoulder. "That crack's been there for ages. It's not growing or anything."

"I'd be afraid it would break open and the ceiling would fall on me in the middle of the night or something."

"I never thought about it," she said. "Now I will. Thanks a lot, Jules."

I laughed. "No problem."

We sat there saying nothing for a while, and then she said, "How's your mom taking it?"

"I don't know. Okay, I guess. She's been sleeping a lot."

She chewed her lip. "Kevin was right. You know, he could tell something was really wrong at the party.

I snorted. "What tipped him off?" I said. "My mom screaming or my dad taking off?"

Megan glared at me. "His parents divorced when he was three. He's been through a lot, too, Julie."

"Sorry," I said. "I didn't mean . . . " My voice trailed off.

Megan stared at the wall; her chin stuck out like a prizefighter's, which she does when she's really mad. "I mean," she said, shaking her head, "he was only trying to help, and you know . . ." She kept shaking her head while I waited for her to finish her sentence.

"Sorry," I finally said again. She kept staring at the wall and shaking her head as I played with the pink flower things sewn onto her bedspread, and neither of us said anything else. The silence was suddenly broken when Rudy yawned, hauled himself to his feet, and stretched right in front of Megan, his back legs quivering—and his stomach lurching!

"Rudy, NO!" I yelled as Megan's eyes went wide with horror. She pulled her legs up, but she was too late—Rudy did a giant heave, and peanut butter-colored puke spewed all over Megan's feet and across her pink-flowered bedspread. She screamed like she was being attacked by an axe murderer.

"YOU STUPID DOG, WHAT IS YOUR PROBLEM?" Mrs. Bartlet must have gone out for a minute, because if she were in the house she would have heard for sure. Megan leaped off the bed—dripping—and still shouting at poor Rudy, and I realized why he hadn't wanted any cookies.

"He couldn't help it," I said. "I mean, I'm sure he didn't want to do it." Just then Rudy burped, and a huge gob of drool dribbled out the side of his mouth and onto her carpet. Megan looked as if she was about to strangle Rudy, but then she turned her gaze on me.

"Julie, get a clue," she said and walked out of the room, slamming the door shut behind her.

As I'm riding home I see trees go by and cars go by, but I can't hear them—all I hear are the pounding

waves. I see Rudy running next to me—running in slow motion, everything in slow motion. A long, black line snakes beside me, and I fly over the edge of it and fall, but I don't scream.

My bike wheel was still spinning when I came to. Rudy was licking my face, and my head ached. I looked around. I was sitting at the bottom of another deep ditch. Cars were whizzing by, but no one could see me because of how deep the ditch was and because of the overgrown weeds growing alongside. Rudy whined and pawed at my leg, and I scratched behind his ears, but my hand was shaking so much that I dropped it and instead rested my head against his side. "It's going to be okay, boy." He was so warm that I dug my fingers into his fur, and then I began to cry.

When I finally hauled my bike out of the ditch, I recognized the road leading to the graveyard on the hill. I wanted to look around, so I walked my bike up the road. Rudy walked beside me nicely the whole way—I couldn't believe it. The gravestones were bleached out and dry looking, as if they were bones themselves, and the words were hard to make out on some of them because they'd been there for so long. At the top of the hill, under a massive tree, one little marker rose crookedly out of the ground. Its words were outlined with that kind of moss that grows on rocks, whatever it's called, and the tree must have protected it from the rain because the letters were really clear.

Here Lies Our Beloved Daughter
Elizabeth Ellen Main.
Born September 9, 1854.
Died November 13, 1856.
"Only a Short Time on Earth,
But in Our Hearts Forever."

Rudy sat quietly as I read it out loud to him. Elizabeth was only two when she died. Nearby were her parents' gravestones—the mother had died in 1870, the father in 1874. "At least they're all together now," I said to Rudy, and he sniffed.

I wondered what Elizabeth had been like. Did she have blonde or brown hair, or red even? Was she chubby? Had she been sickly her whole life (all two years of it)? I wondered how her mom and dad had felt when she died, and then I wondered if anyone else thought of things like that, or if it was just me? I mean, it's as if I saw this little family all together, being so happy, and then one day—

boom—she's gone. I felt pretty sad all the way home, and even though Rudy cut in front of the bike and I almost fell again, I didn't yell at him.

We got home just after dark, and my mom's car was in the driveway. I put my bike in the garage and opened the front door, keeping Rudy close to me because he was looking tired, and I didn't want him doing anything stupid.

"Mom?" I called into the dark and quiet house.

"Hi." Mom was sitting on the couch—I hadn't even seen her! I must have jumped, because Mom said, "What's the matter, Julie? You look as if you've seen a ghost." She didn't move.

"Mom, are you okay?" My heart was pounding, but I don't know why; I mean, why would I be afraid of my own mom? However, I was, and as Rudy leaned against my leg, I thought he might be scared, too.

Mom gave a dry laugh. "Never better, Julie, never better. Sit down," she said, pointing to the end of the couch.

I stayed standing. "Um, Mom," I said. "We kind of need more milk and food and things. I . . . I had to feed Rudy peanut butter for two days, and he . . . he just threw it up. So maybe could you buy some . . . dog food or something?"

There was an unpleasant silence as her stare bored through me like a drill. When she spoke, her voice was low and cut into me. "Julie, I will buy you whatever food you want. Milk, eggs . . . whatever you need. But I . . . won't . . . buy . . . that . . . dog . . . a . . . thing."

I gulped back the tears and walked toward my room like a wooden marionette, with Rudy behind me: one foot in front of the other, one foot in front of the other.

"Julie," Mom said. I stopped, but I did not turn around.

"Your father called. I told him you weren't here, and he didn't leave a message."

CHAPTER FOUR

I lay in bed long after the sun came up, and then I only got up and got dressed because Rudy was whining and scratching at the door. I walked to the sliding doors and let him outside. I noticed that my mom's door was open and her room empty, but she had left a twenty-dollar bill on the table with a note beneath it.

> *Julie, can you pick up a few things for dinner?*
> *I'll be home around 5:30.*
> *Mom*
> *P.S. I need to talk to you about last night.*

I stared at the note for a moment before stuffing it in my pocket and grabbing the phone to call Dad. When the voicemail picked up, I stared at my phone and wanted more than anything to smash it against the wall. Rudy whined at the door, so I let him in and looked in the fridge for something to eat. There was a pot of something with a plate on top, but whatever it was had grown green fuzzy mold.

There was one wrinkly apple in the fruit bowl, so I washed it, cut it in two and tossed half to Rudy (sitting next to me, staring), who caught it mid-air and gulped it down. I was going to eat the other half, but he kept on staring, so I tossed him that, too. He caught it and swallowed without even chewing and stared at me again.

My stomach was still rumbling, so I looked in the cupboard for more food. There was some instant rice, so I cooked that up. I'd never had rice for breakfast before, but it wasn't too bad, and Rudy seemed to like it okay—he licked his bowl and let out a gigantic burp. In fact, he looked so pleased with himself, I laughed, even though I didn't really feel like it. There were mountains of dishes everywhere, and there was laundry, too. Maybe I would do it when I got back.

Rudy and I set off for the store, which was maybe a five-minute walk from the house. He kept pulling on the leash until his tongue was

purple, which kind of reminded me of the day he arrived at the party—not too great.

"Heel, Rudy," I said, jerking the leash up and toward me, the way the training video showed me, but he continued to lunge, and did so all the way to the store.

"You know what I don't get, Rudy?" I said, as I leaned over him to tie his leash to the shop railing. He panted in my face, smiling. "Why are you so good sometimes and so bad other times?" He kept panting and smiling, all the way up until I stepped into the store, and then he screeched like he'd been abandoned or attacked by wild animals. In every aisle of the store I could hear Rudy howling.

"My goodness," one lady said to me. "What on earth is making that racket? Is that someone's *dog*?" I just shrugged and shook my head, as if I was just as disgusted as she was. I walked faster, dumping things into my basket: eggs, bread, butter, milk, and apples. I stopped dead in front of the dog food where a happy collie dog smiled out at me from a small bag. *"Doesn't Your Best Friend Deserve the Very Best?"* the bag declared. It was $4.20, almost a quarter of my entire budget. Just then, Rudy howled extra loud (it was as if he

could read my mind or something), and I decided to put the bag in the basket and worry about what to tell Mom later.

I got into the "Twelve Items or Less" lane, behind a guy who had 14 items on the conveyor, but I decided not to say anything and instead try to add up what I was buying. When I got to the bag of dog food, I got this kind of knot in my stomach—it was going to be tight.

The guy paid and left, and the lady on the register said to me, "Good morning, dear." I smiled, but my lips felt a little shaky, so I didn't say anything. Rudy must have caught sight of me, because he was staring at me through the window, and his breath fogged up the glass.

"Is he yours?" asked the cashier. Just as I nodded, Rudy gave a piercing, high-pitched yowl.

"He's kind of cute," she said. "And he sure seems to love you a lot, doesn't he?"

I looked at Rudy, who was yowling so much I swear I could see foam on the sides of his mouth. "Yeah," I said. "I guess he does."

She finished ringing up my stuff and smiled at me. "That'll be $22.93, dear."

My cheeks got hot as I handed her the twenty. "That's all I've got," I said. "Just take out the butter

or something." I grabbed the butter and held it out to her, my hand shaking a little. She glanced around, as if she didn't want anyone to hear, and leaned toward me. "Don't worry about it," she said. She took the butter from me and put it back in the bag. "Don't you worry about it at all."

"But I . . ."

"I'll pay for it, don't you worry."

"Thank you," I said, trying to smile as tears prickled behind my eyes. I fumbled at the bags as she handed them to me.

"You take care, dear." Then she stood and watched me leave, like a mommy sending her child off on the school bus.

When I untied Rudy, he acted as if I'd left him there for a year, jumping up at me and licking my face, but before we walked home, I kneeled and gave him a huge hug. He got really still and put his head on my shoulder, and we just sat there for a minute.

Somehow I got the bags and Rudy home, but it wasn't easy. Mom still wasn't home, so I put down a bowl of dog food for Rudy, and he kind of dove at it, as if he was starving or something (I guess he really doesn't like peanut butter).

I cleaned the dishes, wiped the table, swept and mopped the kitchen floor, did the laundry, folded the clothes, vacuumed up the dirt, and straightened the living room. It looked really good when I was finished.

I took Rudy to the backyard, and we worked on something for the rest of the afternoon. By the time Mom got home, I had made scrambled eggs and toast, and I laid out a plate of sliced apples on the table for dessert. Mom looked tired when she came in, but when she smelled the toast, it must have made her feel good, because she smiled. She didn't say anything as she looked around the living room, and then she walked into the kitchen and shook her head as if she couldn't believe it.

"Julie, you must have worked all day on this."

I pulled out a chair from the table for her and she sat down slowly, still looking around her— I guess she was really surprised. The toast shot up in the toaster, so I buttered it and stacked the pieces on a plate before spooning the scrambled eggs into a serving dish and setting it out on the table beside the plates and cutlery. Mom just sat there, kind of touching her knife and fork like they had turned into gold or something.

"Would you like milk or water?" I asked her.

"Umm . . . milk, please," she said, still looking like she was in the wrong house.

The whole time Rudy sat restlessly by the couch, and when I looked his way, he stood up, and his eyes seemed to be saying, "Can I come and eat, too? Can I? I'm starving, you know . . ." I held up my hand and stared him down, causing him to slink back onto his haunches.

Mom and I ate our eggs (they were actually pretty good) and our toast. She didn't say much, but I could tell she really liked everything. When we had finished, she took my hand. Her head was bent over so that I couldn't see her face, but I saw a couple of tears plop onto the table.

"I'm sorry, Julie," she said, her voice thick with emotion. I squeezed her hand, and she pulled me in, hugging me to her. I could feel her body shaking as we held on to each other for a long time. Then I felt something bump against me—Rudy had put his head on Mom's knee. She let go of me and stared at him, not mad or upset, just kind of bewildered—sort of like, "Who is this dog and why is he putting his head on my knee?" Mom reached out her hand and slowly scratched him behind his ears, which of course caused Rudy to groan.

"He likes it, Mom," I said. "He likes you." Mom pulled back her hand, her face suddenly hard. "Um, Mom, look what he can do. I worked with him on it all afternoon!" I said quickly. "Rudy!" I held out my fingers as if they were a gun. "Bang!" Rudy dropped to his side and rolled onto his back, his four legs sticking up in the air like road kill.

Even though she didn't want to, Mom laughed. I got Rudy to do it again and again: "Bang!" Each time he'd drop like a rock and poke his legs in the air, and each time Mom couldn't stop herself from laughing; in fact, we both laughed until we cried.

"Enough, enough," she said, holding her side. "Oh, I needed that." She wiped her eyes. "You worked so hard making things right here, and I haven't been here for you at all—thanks for everything."

There was one thing I still had to do, and now seemed like a good moment. "Mom," I said. "I have to tell you something." I couldn't quite look her in the eye. "I . . . I kind of got Rudy some dog food today." She stiffened, and I hurried on. "I mean, I know you said you wouldn't pay for any food, but he really didn't have any, and he was hungry and . . . I'll pay you back; I'll do jobs around the house and mow the lawn . . ."

Mom put her hand up for me to stop, and she looked as if she was thinking about everything really hard as her eyes hovered over me, and then Rudy, and then back over me. She smiled, and I realized I'd been holding my breath in for a while as it whooshed out of me.

"Julie," she said, "you keep buying food for that crazy dog of yours."

You know, I don't think I'd ever loved my mom as much as I did right then.

CHAPTER FIVE

When I got up the next morning, Mom had left a note on the table again, hoping I had a good day and that I was supposed to call her at the bank and let her know if I wanted Indian, Chinese, pizza, or whatever else for dinner. I phoned and left a message on her voicemail saying I wanted Chinese. I tried phoning my dad again, but there was still no answer, and it kind of made me mad, you know? Why did it always have to be me trying to get hold of him? I knew my dad loved me and that he'd call me when he could and that he gets really busy at work, but I still wished he would call.

I phoned Megan, but when her mom answered, I suddenly remembered we weren't talking and hung up. I don't know why I forgot; I just did. She was the one person I talked to about everything, and I didn't really have anyone else to talk to—besides Rudy, of course, but who goes to a dog for advice? I gave him some dog biscuits, which he gulped down like it was his last meal, and then made myself some toast with cinnamon and sugar on it. It tasted really, really good. Rudy, the pig, watched me eating it and licked his lips. I made another piece, drank a glass of milk, and watched TV for a while, but it was pretty boring, so Rudy and I went out in the backyard, not caring that I was still in my pajamas, and we sat on the back step and just hung out, you know?

I closed my eyes and leaned back against the house. There was a sweet smell in the air like fresh hay. It smelled so clean. The birds were singing and there was one that made this *whoo-ee-hooo* sound. I scratched Rudy's head and listened to *whoo-ee-hooo*, over and over. The sun was already warm, and I felt very peaceful, as if, somehow, everything would be okay. Someone started up a lawnmower. It was so loud I couldn't hear the birds singing any more, but the sun was getting pretty hot, and the moment had kind of gone anyway. I got the idea that maybe I could cut our lawn—it was looking really bad—and while

I might not have cut the lawn before, I was pretty sure I could handle it.

"Come on, Rudy, let's go inside," I said, turning to step through the sliding door, and of course he had to go through at the exact same time, so we both got jammed for a second. We struggled for another second, until he squeezed in ahead of me and then danced around, panting and smiling, as if he'd done some great trick. I shook my head at him. "You need to learn some manners, Rudy," I said, but he knew I wasn't really mad. I got out some work clothes—the sort of thing Dad wore when he worked in the garden—tied my hair back in a ponytail, and put on a baseball cap.

We went out to the garage where Dad kept his mower, and I rolled it out onto the driveway. Rudy sniffed it and raised his leg, but I yelled at him, and he slunk off, and sauntered over to one of Mom's rose bushes. I yelled at him again, but he was far enough away that he really didn't care.

"Just don't do that in front of Mom," I told him and he grinned at me. I swear he winked, too. "Crazy dog," I muttered.

I turned back to the mower. There were knobs and pull-cords and no instructions on how to get the thing to work. "This could be harder than I thought, Rudy," I said. He came and stood by me as if he was trying to help me figure it out.

"Need some help?" called our next-door neighbor, who was hanging over the low fence, wiping his head with a rag. He was an older man whose wife had died last year, and I'd never spoken to him much, just "Hi" and "Good morning" and stuff like that.

"Thanks," I said.

"No problem, little lady," he said, like someone out of a cowboy movie or something. He came down his driveway and up ours and opened up the gas cap to look inside the tank. Then he looked in another compartment, for oil I think, and then pressed a button on the motor a couple of times. "This primes it," he said, gripping a lever on the handle. "Now hold down the throttle *while* you pull the cord."

He pulled on the cord, and the engine caught and started up. "Real easy if you know how to do it," he shouted over the noise, winking at me. "Not so easy if you don't." He shut it off. "Now you try it."

I just wanted to get started, not take mowing lessons from some old guy I didn't even know, but he was trying to help, and besides, he'd shut it off, and I had to get it started again. I kind of smiled at him, like gee-I-don't-mind-at-all, and bent down to press the button.

"Pump it two or three times," he said. I pumped the button and pulled back on the cord, but the engine barely rattled. A sweat broke out on my forehead.

"No, no, you forgot to hold down the throttle. Try it again."

This guy was beginning to get on my nerves, but I gripped the throttle, took a deep breath, and yanked on the cord, and the engine snarled into life.

"Whoa!" I said, jumping back with a big, dumb grin on my face. I know it sounds stupid, but I was so proud I'd started it—as if I'd discovered a cure for cancer or something.

"Now you know how to start a lawnmower all by yourself," he shouted and waved as he turned and walked back to his garden. Somehow I just knew that he'd seen that whole thing with my parents right before Dad left—and probably all the fights before that, too.

Mowing the lawn is hard work. It's not so much pushing the mower around—that's nothing—it's making sure you don't miss any parts so your lawn doesn't look as if it's had a bad haircut. I had to crisscross around quite a bit, but I thought it looked pretty good for a first try. When I'd rolled the lawnmower back into the garage, I noticed that Mom's flowers looked dry, so I uncoiled the hose and turned the tap on all the way. I guess it was too much, however, because the hose erupted with water, flopping around like a possessed snake. Rudy lunged at it, grabbing it in his teeth and shaking it (he probably thought he was protecting me) until it sprang about a million holes.

"Oh great!" I shouted. "Just great, you big, dumb dog." I grabbed the hose and blasted him with water while he gulped and snapped at the spray like he was having an attack or something. He looked so silly, I laughed until my sides hurt. I was dancing back and forth, too, and I guess it must have been pretty slippery, because I slipped and landed on my back. Rudy pounced on me and slobbered all over my face, which is pretty gross, I guess, but I was laughing so hard I didn't care. As we were rolling around on the wet grass, I noticed Brianna, Suze, and Jessica walking by.

"Stop it, Rudy," I shouted, pushing him away and sitting up. "Hey," I called.

The three of them stopped. "Hi, Julie," said Jessica and Brianna, but Suze was looking away, as if there was something very, very interesting in the distance. I tried to get up, but Rudy bowled me over again, furiously wagging his tail. "That's enough!" I said, pushing him off. His ears went back, and he slunk to the ground.

I finally got up, pulled my wet clothes into some sort of order, and got my hair out of my eyes. "So what are you guys up to?" I asked. Suze kept studying whatever it was she found so fascinating, but she didn't say anything.

"Just hanging around," muttered Jessica, and Brianna shrugged halfheartedly. Suddenly I felt as if I had the plague.

"Is something wrong?" I asked.

Suze smiled this prissy smile that made me want to slap her, and she still wouldn't look at me. Brianna stared at the ground. "See you, Julie," she said.

Three girls walk away, down the long street, leaving just one, a leafless tree, alone. Everything tilts—the ocean, the tree—but the dog holds me rooted to the ground with his soft, brown eyes.

I changed back into my pajamas, even though the sun was still up, and curled up on the couch. Rudy jumped up and settled in where my legs were bent, falling asleep right away, but I couldn't sleep, even though I was tired. I kept thinking about things, thoughts buzzing in my head until I almost felt dizzy, but I don't even know what I was thinking about. There was this hollow space inside me, as if someone had carved out a piece, and I was just lying there, thinking about stuff I didn't even care about. The phone rang, so I shook Rudy off, and he slunk away down the hall as I ran to answer it.

"Hello?" I said.

"Baby! Finally I've got you on the phone."

"Dad! I . . ."

"Listen, babe, I don't have time to talk right now, but how about I swing by on Saturday and pick you up for the weekend. What do you say?"

"I'd love that!"

"And don't worry about Evie, baby. She wants to meet you, so don't worry about it."

I had forgotten about Evie. "Are you sure it's okay?"

"Sure I am, baby, but leave that dog of yours at home."

"Dad," I said, "I *can't* leave Rudy here. Mom would never agree to that."

There was a silence, and my gut tightened. "Dad, please. I really want to see you. I haven't seen you since . . . well, you know."

There were a few more seconds of silence, and then he muttered something I didn't catch. "Yeah, bring it then," he said with a sigh. "I'll say something to Evie. I love you, babe."

"I love you, too, Dad."

The phone went dead, so I called him right back because I didn't even know what time he was coming or anything. There was no answer, but it didn't matter at all because he had called, and I was finally going to see him again!

"Rudy, guess what?" I called. "Hey, where are you?" I heard a thump (he must have jumped off my bed), and he came running out into the hall, wagging his tail like he was trying to take off. "We finally get to see Dad . . . We finally get to see Dad!" I sang.

I grabbed his front paws, and we were dancing around the living room when my mom asked, "What's the occasion?" She was standing in the front doorway, holding a big bag with a greasy stain spreading up its side. I dropped Rudy's paws and suddenly felt guilty, you know, as if I'd been caught stealing or something. "Um, Dad just called, and he's picking me up on Saturday."

It was as if my mom was suddenly carved out of stone: her eyes went flinty, her jaw got hard, and her mouth creased into a bitter line.

"Your father should have asked me first if it was okay," she said, spitting out the words. "I had plans for us to go to the movies and spend some time together." She kept staring at me, but I didn't know what she wanted from me. "But if you really want to go . . . then go."

"I do," I said. "I really do. But," I added quickly, "I also really want to spend time with you. I just haven't seen him for so long, you know?" Mom nodded without saying anything. "Maybe we can go out during the week, or something, or maybe next weekend?" Mom nodded again and put the bag of food on the table.

The day is so clear, I feel as if I can jump off the mountain and fly. The mountain range gathers around me—beautiful, white-robed, and pristine. The ocean looms far below me, and while I know it

is there, I do not look down—I refuse to look down. Still, my feet slip, and I fall headfirst toward the ink that swirls like a thick whirlpool, toward its dark, gurgling center. I try to scream, but my voice sticks in my throat. I fall, and I cannot scream.

CHAPTER SIX

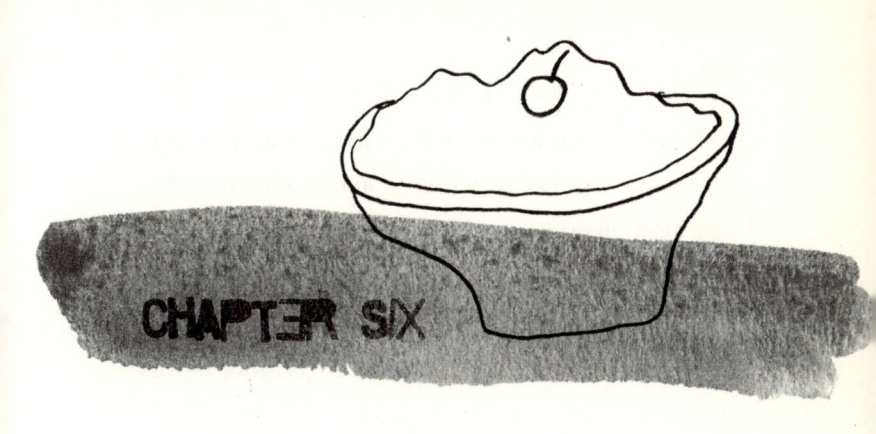

"Well, that's it," I said to Rudy, who stood with his nose in my suitcase, snuffling. My bag was packed: toothbrush and toothpaste, hairbrush, five pairs of underwear, five pairs of socks, two pairs of jeans (I was wearing the third pair), and four shirts, not including the one I had on. I thought about what to do just in case they didn't have a TV, so I threw a book in my bag, too. Rudy (who was still snuffling) gave a gigantic, wet snort, like he'd inhaled pepper or something, and stared at me. I looked back at him for a second before it dawned on me. "Oh yeah!" I said and ran into the kitchen, Rudy scrambling after me on the tile floor. I got his dog food and grabbed his leash. "Can't forget about you, right, boy?" Rudy panted and wagged his tail, his eyes forming half-moons.

I made my bed, did the dishes, wiped the table, and even vacuumed the living room, making sure all the strokes on the carpet went in one direction, the way Mom liked it.

It was 10:30 a.m. on Saturday, and Mom had gone before I got up. She left a note saying to call if I wanted to, and that she loved me; it was nice.

I tried calling Dad to see what time he was coming, but there was no answer.

I wanted to talk to Megan so badly, and I couldn't even remember why we'd fought—because Rudy threw up? It seemed like a dumb reason to stay mad, so I picked up the phone and dialed her number.

"Hello," she said.

"Megan? It's Julie."

"Hi."

"Umm . . . Megan, I just wanted to say sorry again for everything the other day. I . . . hope you got the vomit out of everything."

There was silence, and then Megan sighed and said, "That's okay, Jules. Sorry I went off on you like that, but you know Kevin has been going through some hard times, and you kind of hurt my feelings."

What about my hard times, I wanted to say, but I didn't, and instead I said, "Yeah, I'm really sorry."

"Maybe you can come over later," she said.

"Oh, I can't. My dad's coming to get me for the weekend, but I can come over when I get back, okay?"

"Okay. Bye."

"Bye."

I hung up and thought about whether I felt better or sadder. It was crazy, I know, but I felt as if Megan was a stranger sometimes, even though I've known her since forever. Now, it was 10:45—only fifteen minutes had passed. I tried calling Dad again, but there was no answer.

I can't remember what I did all morning and afternoon, though I think I worked on more tricks with Rudy (I would show Dad the "Bang" one, too), and he did okay. Finally—it was maybe 4:30 or something—I heard Dad's truck. I shrieked and ran to the window, scaring Rudy because he jumped off the couch, and I swear his fur stood on end. Dad's truck was outside, and he was honking the horn.

"Come on, babe!" he shouted out the window.

I ran across the grass with my suitcase, like in a slow-motion movie, and I could see his smile, see his face, and hear his voice.

I was halfway into the truck when I noticed Rudy had stopped in the middle of the lawn. "Rudy," I called, but he didn't move. *"Rudy!"*

He walked slowly to the truck, skirting around the front to where I was standing with the door open. "What's wrong with you?" I asked him. "Get in!"

"Crazy mutt!" said Dad, as Rudy scrambled into the back, and I settled down with my suitcase balanced on my lap. Dad leaned over and grabbed me in his arms. "Baby, it's so good to see you. I missed you."

You know, I couldn't say a thing, my throat felt so tight; I was so happy.

He stroked my hair, and I guess I started to cry even though I didn't mean to; it just kind of happened. I cried so hard that snot hung down off my nose in a string, and my eyes felt hot and swollen.

"I'm sorry," I said, and I did a lame attempt at a laugh (my nose was so clogged, I blew out a snot bubble).

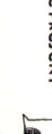

"Hey, don't be stupid; it's okay," he said, laughing. He wiped my cheek with his sleeve, took my chin in his hand, and looked me in the eyes. "I'm here, so everything's okay now" Then he put his truck into gear, and we roared off. It was one of the happiest moments of my life.

Ten minutes later we pulled into the driveway of a small, white house surrounded by tall pines, with a few green shrubs shaped like puffballs thrown in for good measure. A basket of blood-red flowers hung outside the front door, and as I looked around, I realized the nearest neighbor was a minute down the street. I stood in the doorway, Rudy beside me, holding my suitcase.

"Evie?" Dad called before standing beside me, waiting and listening.

"Just a minute," called a voice. A door opened, and a woman as short as me came out (only she was way prettier). Her auburn hair was curled and styled like a shampoo model's and her eyes were a beautiful green moss color (it doesn't sound pretty, but it was, believe me), and she reminded me of a tiny, perfect cat. She held out a delicate, white hand that I grasped, and I think babbled my name. With golf-ball swollen eyes and dried snot all over my face,

I'm sure I looked fabulous, but she smiled as if I was the sweetest thing since bees invented honey.

"It's nice to meet you, Julie," she said and smiled even wider, showing small, perfect (of course), pearly-white teeth. Then she bent down to Rudy and patted his head. Rudy snarled and curled up his lip.

"Rudy!" I said, smacking his nose and causing him to yelp. Evie pulled back, and this look flashed in her eyes and was quickly gone. I couldn't even swear I'd seen it, but I felt a stab of fear in the pit of my stomach.

She smiled at me, shaking her head. "Dogs are so unpredictable, aren't they?"

At dinner, Evie chewed her food in this round, circular way, kind of like the way a cow chews its cud, but somehow she made it look good. She kept looking at my father and smiling, with her head kind of tilted to one side. Rudy had been banished to the far corner, where he sat staring at Evie. We were having pork chops with potatoes and some sort of green vegetable.

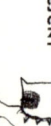

"This is delicious," I said to Evie, just to be polite, because actually I was having trouble chewing the pork, which was really tough.

"Thank you, Julie," she said as she took another pork chop from the platter, put it on my plate, and smiled at me with her white teeth. "Have another."

"Yeah, Julie likes her food—don't you, babe?" Dad elbowed me in the ribs, and Evie laughed her high, tinkling laugh. I looked at him, but he smiled fondly back because he didn't have a clue that he'd said anything insulting. He looked like a kid at Christmas, with Evie on one side and the-daughter-who-likes-her-food on the other. Evie watched and smiled, looking like a saint in a cathedral as I ate each bite. I don't know how, but I even managed to choke down that stupid second pork chop.

"I have a surprise for dessert," Evie said as she got up from the table, and it was at that exact moment that I noticed that Rudy wasn't in his corner.

Evie called from the kitchen. "I made this just for—" There was a crash, followed by, *"YOU IDIOT DOG!"*

Rudy came hurtling out of the kitchen, his face covered in a white foam that was either whipped cream or proof that he had rabies. Then Evie followed, holding a large bowl, with spatters of cream and red gooey stuff smeared down its sides. "I . . . I'm so sorry," I said as Dad and I stared at the bowl, wide-eyed.

Evie took a deep breath and smiled her tight, pearly smile before shaking her head in a what-can-you-do-with-that-stupid-dog kind of way and turning to my dad. "It seems Julie's dog has eaten our dessert." The tinkling laugh sounded again. "You're out of luck, partner!"

My dad looked at her and then at Rudy, who was licking cream off his lips, and burst out laughing. "Man, oh man! That dog is something else!" He slapped his knee and looked at Rudy, but Evie was looking straight at me.

"Don't worry, Evie; I'll go out and get something," Dad said, still laughing as he grabbed his keys and made for the door.

"Dad, wait!" I called, but the door had slammed behind him.

Evie walked toward me, her eyes never leaving my face as she stopped directly in front of me. "You think you're funny?" she asked, a little smile playing on her lips and her green eyes drilling into me.

"Umm, no. I didn't know Rudy was . . ."

"You know what? You are a stupid little girl." Evie leaned in so close I could smell her perfume. She reached up her hand, on which each long nail was painted a perfect, glossy red, and tucked a wisp of hair behind my ear, which caused my heart to hammer in my chest and caused Rudy to growl at her from the corner.

Just then my dad walked back in. "Forgot my wallet," he said but stopped as soon as he saw the two of us. "Uh, everything okay?"

"Perfect," Evie said, smiling. "I was fixing Julie's hair."

I tried to speak, you know I really did try, but my voice wouldn't come out, so I looked at my dad and tried to make my eyes scream, *Don't leave me!*

"You go, Charlie. We'll be fine." Evie smiled at me. "We'll have some girl time. Right, Julie?" She winked at me, and Dad had already turned back to the door. "Oh, and Charlie, honey?" she said. "Take that dog with you."

I heard the truck leave but not Evie, who was silent as she moved behind me. The hairs on my neck stood straight up, but I couldn't move.

"Julie," she whispered in my ear, "this is *my* house." Something crashed behind me, and

I jumped as slivers of glass skittered across the floor.

"That was my favorite," said Evie, sounding disgusted. "My grandmother gave it to me—irreplaceable!"

Something flew by my ear, shattering against the wall in front of me. "That was worth six hundred dollars!" she said.

I shook my head. "Please," I stammered, but she only snorted as she walked around to stand in front of me.

"You won't know what hit you, little girl."

I watch from the ceiling, and I feel concern for the girl but also glad it's not me.

Why does the girl just stand there, rooted to the spot? Why can't she open her mouth and say something, anything?

"What happened?" asked my dad as he opened the door and broken glass crunched beneath his feet. "EVIE," he cried, going to the woman huddled against the wall, weeping. Rudy stood in the doorway, whining. The broken glass circled me like a ring of thorns. "Evie, baby, tell me what happened."

She whimpered, clutching at his shirt and burying her face in his chest, pointing a shaking, perfect, clawed finger at me. "She . . . she's crazy!"

I ride in the truck as the ocean beats in my head and he screams, "Tell me why you did it, just tell me why." His fist punches the steering wheel, and drops of spit fly from his mouth. One lands on my hand, but I say nothing and instead watch the bubble of spit slowly dry from the edges toward its center as Rudy whines gently behind me.

CHAPTER SEVEN

You'd think I'd run home, crying to Mom or Megan, but I didn't tell anybody what happened. I just couldn't bring myself to because it was like I had something to be ashamed of, you know? Part of me wondered, what would make a grown woman do something like that. The only answer I could think of was that I must have asked for it somehow. Of course, another part of me immediately followed with, *Don't be stupid.*

I wanted to be alone and have time to think about things, so I got out my bike on Sunday morning and rode to the cemetery with Rudy in tow. I didn't call Megan or my dad, and Mom was still in her room, so I didn't have to wake her up. As I cycled along, Rudy ran beside me, and he didn't swerve in front like last time; he just ran right next to me. You know, Rudy is a really smart dog, but he only learns fast when he wants to.

I thought about everything Evie had done and how she'd said I'd broken her stuff—as if one minute I could be perfectly normal and the next minute go completely insane and toss glass ornaments around. I mean, how could that make sense to anyone, because it certainly doesn't to me? I have never thrown things (well, maybe when I was, like, two or something), but my dad somehow doesn't even know me well enough to understand that his gross new girlfriend is lying? The fact that he believed her over me really hurt my feelings, and it made me mad and wonder why I hadn't said something.

I pedaled so hard—I guess because I was angry—that Rudy was foaming at the mouth, so I slowed down a little. We got to the old graveyard, and it was like walking into a bubble: no traffic noise, only birds singing and a smell of sweet hay in the air. I found a spot on the hill that wasn't too near a grave and lay down spread-eagled on the grass. Rudy settled next to me, his panting slowing, until he lowered his head and flopped on his side while I just breathed for a while and watched clouds shift in the sky.

I felt like a small dot on the side of a huge ball, as if I was connected to the universe, and I know it sounds stupid, but sometimes I think that, when things are really, really bad, you find something good inside that you didn't know was there before. Maybe it takes something horrible to wake it up, you know? I can't really explain it, but it just seemed like at that moment I understood everything, such as how my parents had screwed up, and that none of this was my fault. I also understood that right now my life really stank, but deep, deep inside I knew I was meant for something better than this.

After a while we got up and wandered around the tombstones. I've always liked imagining what people were like who lived a long time ago, so when we were walking around, I made up stories about people buried there.

"Well, you know, Rudy," I said, "when young *Thomas Alistair McCready* was in his prime, he sailed the seven seas and brought spices back from . . ." I looked at Rudy, who was listening intently. "Where *do* spices come from?" I asked, but Rudy tilted his head at me as if to say, "Duh . . . I don't know."

"Okay, young Thomas brought back *treasure* and an untold fortune and buried it, and to this day there are those who believe that the treasure lies buried with young Tom himself . . ." I really started getting into it. "And then there was the notorious *Willard Ebenezer Morrison*, a scoundrel and ne'er-do-well." We strolled to another marker. "And here," I waved my arm toward the stone like a tour guide, "lies the sickly yet devastatingly handsome *Isaac Baldwin Jackson.*" Rudy sniffed the stone and lifted his leg. "Geez, Rudy," I said. "Show some respect."

I rested my hand on top of another gravestone. "And, of course, we must not forget the stalwart *Frances Price O'Neill*, upon whose back the nations of the free world stand." I had no idea what all that actually meant, but it sounded good, and Rudy seemed to like it. We came to Elizabeth's grave where tall, weedy grass gathered around the headstone, leaning in the breeze that swept up the hill, making the leaves of the tree overhead shift and shimmer. I sat down and stared at the grave, and Rudy looked at me expectantly. "You want to hear about Elizabeth?" He winked at me, so I took that as a yes.

It had to be special for little Elizabeth, so I thought for a minute. "Baby Elizabeth was born a healthy, chubby-cheeked cherub, and should have had a life of utter, unending joy, but her parents, though honest folk, were poor and couldn't spend money on frivolities such as new shoes and a proper coat and hat. And so it was that, in the chilly November of 1856, little Elizabeth caught a cold. 'It will go away,' said her mother. 'She's as strong as an ox,' said her father. Alas, it was not so, and when poor Elizabeth died of her cold, her mother and father turned their tear-filled eyes toward the cruel heavens and realized what a gift their precious child had been, now to be an angel forever more."

And you know what? I started to choke myself up, and Rudy put his head on my knee as I sobbed out baby Elizabeth's concocted story. I was in full swing when a voice behind me asked, "Uh . . . are you okay?"

I screamed like the star in a horror movie and whipped around. Rudy scrambled to his feet, woofing and snarling, but not really being convincing, because he looked kind of scared, too. A guy, probably a little older than me, stood staring like I'd sprouted five heads. His hands were up in front of him as if to say "I-come-in-peace," but for someone who had heard me crying and gabbing to myself, he didn't look too freaked out.

"Oh," I said, wiping a smear of snot across my cheek. "I was just . . ." I didn't even finish because it would have sounded too lame.

"How do you know all that stuff?" he asked.

I thought about lying, saying I was a junior historian or that Elizabeth was my great-great-grandmother (except that she died when she was two), but instead I said, "I made it up."

"Okay," he said, drawing the word out as he stared at me like he was contemplating whether or not to run. However, he just shrugged. "That's cool. Doesn't matter to me. Name's Jordan." He stuck out his hand and then quickly pulled it back when he saw my slime-encrusted hand.

"Yeah, sorry," I said, wiping it on the grass. "I'm Julie, and this ferocious beast is Rudy." Rudy panted at him, smiling. Jordan bent down and let his hand be sniffed by Rudy, who then allowed Jordan to scratch him behind the ears. "Anyway, what are you doing here in a graveyard, crying like that?"

"I don't know." Usually I'd feel kind of embarrassed talking about stuff like that with a stranger, so I didn't say anything else for a second, but Jordan looked at me as he scratched Rudy's ears, waiting, as if he really wanted to hear the answer.

I shrugged. "I guess it's been a pretty tough summer. My dad left my mom and me a couple of weeks ago."

Jordan shook his head. "Man, that *is* rough. My sister's husband left her and her kid, and she's living at home again in our basement. My mom and dad help her out, but still . . ." He let the sentence hang in the air, and then smiled at me before squinting into the sun. "I usually help take care of my nephew, but today I didn't have to." He sat down next to me, and then scratched out a pebble from the dirt and lobbed it lazily into the air. It landed near the bottom of the hill, rolling to a stop.

"Where do you live?" I asked.

He pointed in the same direction Megan lived in. "Down the hill, right through those trees. First brick house." He hesitated for a moment. "I come up here a lot because . . ." he said, shrugging. "I don't know. I like it. It's peaceful."

I nodded. "Yeah. I like it, too." We looked out over the hill, not saying anything for a while, but it wasn't a silence where you want to start giggling because you feel so stupid. It was comfortable, you know, and though I could see the snake of road skirting along the bottom of the hill, up there I felt higher than the clouds.

The sun was getting low over the horizon. "I've got to go," I said. "I live over that way," and pointed toward town.

"Maybe I'll see you around, Julie," said Jordan. "See you, Rudy. You're a good dog." He stroked Rudy's head, and Rudy licked his hand.

"Yeah," I said. "See you around." Halfway down, he waved but kept on walking.

CHAPTER EIGHT

Mom was lying on the couch when I got home. I said hello, and she rolled over and smiled.

"Julie," she said and held out her arms to me, so I leaned over to hug her.

"Uh . . . Mom, you said you wanted to go to the movies. Do you still want to? There's a . . ."

"No," she whispered. "No." She waved her hand in front of her face like she was batting away a pesky fly.

I stared at her for a minute. "Are you okay?"

She snorted. "Am I okay? Am I?" She looked at me, and then she flipped herself around so she faced the couch and not me. "I'm fine," she muttered.

I gritted my teeth against the tears that filled my eyes. I had thought I was pretty strong after what happened with my dad and Evie, but

I couldn't take any more, and I totally lost it. I started yelling at her.

"Who do you think you are, leaving me alone like this? Dad left me, too, and I'm going through this, too, not just you!" And you know the big response I got? Nothing. I felt like shaking her until she dealt with her problems, instead of zoning out and leaving me here alone. My heart felt as if it was going to burst in my chest, and I was breathing really fast. I took Rudy and went out for a walk to keep myself from exploding into a million pieces.

The stars were out, and I bitterly wondered how they could be out, twinkling, and how the moon could be up in the sky like everything was so normal when it was all just one big lie. I sat down on the curb and rocked back and forth, shaking my head, trying to get away from myself. Rudy leaned against me, his head on my knee, looking up at me with sad, brown eyes.

"You're my only friend," I said, and hugged him so hard he began to whimper and wriggle. Eventually, I had to go home because there was nowhere else to go. Mom was still draped across the couch, so I silently crept into the kitchen, got the phone, and took Rudy with me to my room before jamming a chair under the door handle. I flopped on my bed and called Megan.

"Hi, Julie. Isn't it kind of late?"

I didn't even know what time it was, so I looked at my alarm clock—11:15 p.m. "Sorry . . . I just really need to talk to someone," I said, and then I got choked up and couldn't get another word out, you know?

"Jules, what's wrong?" She must have asked me a dozen times.

Finally I managed to speak. "My mom is lying on the couch doing nothing, and I was supposed to go to my dad's this weekend, but his girlfriend . . ." I couldn't talk again.

Megan was silent for a moment before saying, "I'm really sorry, Jules, and it's so weird that you had problems, too, because actually Kevin had this problem with *his* mom this weekend and he's kind of bummed about it, too."

For a second I stared at the phone, unable to believe it. "Megan," I said, almost shouting. "I don't care what happened to Kevin, okay? This is happening to *me*!" Megan started to say something, but I cut her off. "You act like you don't even care! All you talk about is Kevin. Well,

I've got my own problems to worry about, and I'm sick of nobody caring about what—"

There was a click, and the line went dead. She hung up on me? I screamed into the phone, "I never liked Kevin anyway!" and threw it at the wall.

I lie curled on my bed, and the room swirls around me, a carousel of ink-black shadows. I am lost in a dark room without a door.

The weak morning light peered through my blinds. I had no idea how long I'd slept, and Rudy was pawing at the door, needing to go out. I groaned, and he scratched again and whined. "Okay, okay. I'm coming," I said, hoisting myself off the bed. My head felt like it was three feet wide, and every bit of it throbbed.

Out in the living room, Mom was still lying on the couch, which was bad because it was Monday morning, and she was still here. I looked at the clock on the stove—10:45 a.m.!

"Mom. Get up!" She rolled over and grunted. "Mom, get up! You're late for work!" I pulled on her arm, and behind me, Rudy decided he had waited long enough and that the living room carpet was as good as the backyard.

"RUDY!" He didn't stop; instead, he quivered and whined until he was finished, which seemed to take a very long time.

"Mom! GET UP!" I yelled, running for paper towels. Rudy ran after me, snapping at my heels and barking—he must have thought I was playing a game or something. I stopped in the kitchen to catch my breath, and Rudy skidded into the back of my leg. I was biting my lip to keep from screaming my head off as I looked at Rudy, panting, smiling, and utterly clueless. I was cleaning up after Rudy when Mom sat up and wrinkled her nose. "What's that terrible smell?" she asked, sniffing.

"Don't worry about it, Mom," I replied, snapping a little. I mean, I realize she's my mom, but I'd had it, you know?

Her bleary eyes grew wide. "I . . . I'm late?" She looked around blinking.

"It's 10:45. No wait, 10:53 now."

She tried to get off the couch, but her leg was trapped by a blanket, so I went over and ripped it off.

"I . . . I have to . . . I . . . I need to . . ." She got off the couch and ran one way, stopped, turned, and ran the other. I would have laughed, but it really wasn't funny, especially when she stepped in the puddle in the living room carpet.

"Ugh!" She screamed and held up her foot, staring at it like it had been dipped in acid.

"It's nothing, Mom. Go take a shower, okay?" It felt was like she was eight years old, and I was the mom. When I heard the shower running, I called Mom's work. "This is Julie Walker, Claire's daughter. I wanted to let you know that my mom woke up feeling ill this morning, but she's feeling much better now, and she told me to tell you she's on her way." Whoever took the message thanked me for calling and called me "dear."

I banged on the bathroom door. "Come on, you've got to get out and go."

She came out dripping, wrapped in a towel, looking only slightly more clear-eyed. "Coffee," she muttered.

"I'll get it," I said. "You get dressed." I put in an extra scoop of coffee into the machine, just to make sure it was strong enough. When the coffee was done, I poured the whole pot, black, into a giant travel mug, and carried it with both hands into Mom's room. Surprisingly, she had managed to get dressed and sort of dry her hair—well, it was dry enough, anyway. As she was putting in earrings, she actually looked like Mom again.

"Wow!" she said, taking the mug from me. "That's a lot of coffee. Thanks, Julie. What would I do without you?"

I managed a tight-lipped smile, but everything I thought of to say could wait until later. I stared at her pretty coldly, and I could see I was hurting her feelings, but I didn't care, if you want to know the truth. She ducked her head, closed her eyes, and nodded.

When Mom was nearly out the door, she turned to me. "I'm sorry," she said, and her eyes looked so sad. When she tried to hug me, I didn't hug her back; I felt like a wooden soldier, my arms glued to my sides.

She managed a sad smile and said, "I love you, Julie." I watched from behind the living room curtains as she got into her car, where she sat for a moment, wiping tears from her cheeks, before driving away.

CHAPTER NINE

On one hand, I felt like a cold-hearted witch by treating my own mom that way, but in the other hand, I didn't feel *that* bad. I thought it was time the adults started acting like adults, not me. I was supposed to be the kid, you know? Okay, I was fourteen and pretty mature for my age, but still. As far as Megan was concerned, I didn't care if I never talked to her again. I mean, I call her in the middle of the night, in the middle of a *crisis*, and she starts talking about *Kevin*? I wasn't even sure who she was any more, and maybe I didn't care anyway. I think Rudy wanted to go for a walk because he kept staring at me, but I was too angry, so I paced back and forth in the living room while he watched me. He looked like he was watching a tennis match, but it didn't make me laugh; it just annoyed me.

"Rudy, go and lie down or something!" He didn't move until I stomped my foot right in front of his face. He slunk away and disappeared into my room.

I decided I was going to talk to Mom and Dad. I'd talk to Mom tonight, but today I'd write Dad a letter. Dad had taken his computer, so I ripped some lined paper from one of my old school notebooks, sat at the kitchen table, and wrote.

Dad,

I need to write to you and tell you about what really happened at Evie's. She was the one who broke everything, not me. I swear that when you left she just started throwing things and going kind of crazy. I don't know why she did it, but she said something like, "You're in my house now, stupid girl." I can't remember exactly.

I actually feel really angry that you think I could do that. I mean, I'm your daughter, and if you don't know me by now, then I must be a terrible daughter or something. I don't even know what to say to you.

Julie

P.S. I still love you, and while I don't know if you still love me, I hope you at least believe me because I'm telling the truth.

Dad's a construction foreman and always on a job site, but I knew that if I delivered it to the office, they would make sure he got it. Rudy and I started out. I thought I was pretty sure of the way, but things look different when you're riding a bike instead of sitting in a car. Anyway, I got turned around, and by the time we finally got there, I swear it was almost going-home time. I tied Rudy's leash to a lamppost outside (he started yowling immediately) and then gave the letter to the lady behind the reception desk who promised me Dad would get it first thing in the morning, and what was that awful noise?

By the time I rescued Rudy, he was foaming again. I was really hungry, but I hadn't brought any money. I decided we couldn't afford to get lost on the way back, so I was staring at the street signs for a minute, and suddenly a young girl of around six or seven walked by with her mom and dad. She was between them, holding each of their hands and looking up at them with a look on her face like you-two-are-the-best-parents-ever. She was skipping and singing, and

I could tell she really thought it would be like that forever. She kind of reminded me of myself at that age, or maybe it was just that I would have given anything to be that little girl for one small second.

I didn't get too lost on the way home, so we were back before dark, which was lucky. I wasn't ready to face Mom yet, so Rudy and I sat on the front step. I scratched behind his ears, and he nestled his head into my lap and got pretty comfortable. I hadn't been paying much attention to him because I'd been mad all day, and mad at him, too, even though he hadn't really done anything. I felt kind of guilty about that, so when he started to drool on my leg, I didn't even make him move his head. The sun was setting and the streetlights were just flickering on when Mom opened the door.

"Julie," she said, but I didn't turn around. "Julie, can we talk?" she said again, but I continued to ignore her. "Julie, answer me! No matter what's happened, I'm still your mother, so—"

"Then act like it!" I shouted, flinging myself around to face her and knocking Rudy off my lap. "If you're still my mom, why don't you . . ." I burst out crying so hard, the tears flung out into the air like confetti. I'd never spoken to my mom like that before.

"Julie . . ." I felt her arms around me, and I didn't move for a second. Then my arms flew around her, and we just kind of clung to each other.

"Julie," she said, "forgive me."

Of course. Yes.

The next morning I felt filled with light, like how the next day after a terrible storm is sunny and clear, and you can't get over how beautiful it all is, you know what I mean? My mom made it to work, and I felt like I could breathe for the first time in a week. I had delivered the letter to my dad so that he would understand, and I felt good about that, too. Maybe things were going to be okay after all; they couldn't have got much worse.

I played with Rudy in the backyard, and then we both went for a swim. Rudy had been chasing me around the garden, snapping at my heels. When he does that, I can't help but scream, you know? Maybe a caveman part of my brain remembers being chased, even though I know Rudy wouldn't hurt me. Anyway, I jumped into the pool to escape and he, of course, dived in right on top of me.

"Geez, Rudy," I spluttered, "you're going to drown me!" He didn't seem too concerned, paddling around me in circles with this big grin on his face and his fur sticking up in spikes on his head. He looked so stupid; I could hardly keep treading water because I was laughing so hard. I tossed a floating tennis ball to the other end of the pool, and he lunged ferociously after it.

"Good boy!" I said. "Now bring it here." Of course he ignored me, so I swam after him, trying to get the ball, but he kept moving it from one side to the other with his mouth, keeping it just out of my reach.

"I command you to bring it to me!" I said, in what I thought was a stern, authoritarian voice, just like the training video recommended, but he must have thought I said "paddle away faster!" or something, because that's exactly what he did. I climbed out of the pool and ran around the edge until I reached him. "INCOMING," I shrieked, as he tried frantically to paddle away, and I dropped on him and clung to him like I was barrel riding. I finally got that ball from his stupid jaws, and when I did, I hoisted it in triumph, like I had just won at the Olympics or something.

At that moment I saw my dad watching from the gate. Rudy snatched the ball from my hand and swam away. Suddenly I felt cold, so I swam to the edge, climbed out, and stood there, waiting. I guess Rudy saw I wasn't playing any more, or maybe he knew something was up, because he scrambled out of the pool and came running over to stand by me, dripping. Dad walked over slowly. He had circles under his eyes, and his hair was uncombed. When he came over to greet us, Rudy shook himself dry right next to him.

"Stupid mutt!" said Dad. Followed quickly by, "Sorry." He sat heavily on a deckchair. "Got your note," he said, looking at the ground. "I don't know what to say." He ran his hands through his hair before looking around and grabbing another deckchair. "Here, baby, sit down." I sat down stiffly, and as he took my hand, I swear I saw tears in his eyes. I'd never seen him cry before. "Baby, I know you're angry, and I know it hasn't been easy for you with your mom and me." He rubbed his free hand over his face, shaking his head. "If

I could change things, I would. You know that, don't you?"

I sat like a statue, not speaking.

"I . . . I thought I knew how things were, but then, when you acted like that, I could see that this separation was really . . ."

When you acted like that . . . When you acted like that . . . The ocean surges in my head, crashing, spinning. He doesn't believe me . . . He doesn't believe me.

Dad buried his face in his hands. "I just don't know why you did it, baby. If you were hurting that much . . ." He shook his head. "And then writing that letter? I mean, that just made it worse."

"GET OUT!" I scream. "GET OUT!" I lunge at him with my own small claws, but he grabs my puny hands, tears shining on his cheeks. He lets go, and I fall like a tumbling leaf, over my dog and land, silently, on my back while thick clouds skitter across the blue-jewel sky.

CHAPTER TEN

I sat at Elizabeth's grave, yanking out the weeds that clustered around the headstone. I hadn't played with Rudy, and I hadn't spoken to Mom last night, so I don't know what she thought. Maybe she thought I was still angry with her because I wouldn't come out of my room for dinner.

"Julie, please," she'd said, but I just stared at the ceiling, not wanting to listen. Rudy scratched at my door, but I wouldn't let him in, either. And then this morning, I left him at home and rode alone to the graveyard. He watched me leave from the living room window, his eyes sad and confused.

There were dark clouds overhead, but I didn't care. I lay back and stretched out my arms, running my hands over the grass. What a fool I'd been to think things couldn't get worse; things could always get worse. What a fool I'd been to think my dad would believe me. My heart felt like a stone in my chest, and I couldn't even cry. The good things I'd felt were meant for me, the dreams I'd had about being happy—it all seemed so childish. I held on to the earth, and together we turned under a sky that threatened rain.

I slip off the rock and fall head first into the black, gurgling center. I hit the water, and ink fills my nostrils, my eyes, and my mouth. I struggle and paw at the thick, black water, try to see which way is up, but I cannot see . . . I cannot see . . .

"JULIE." Someone shook my shoulder, and I heard the sound of sobbing. To my surprise, it was me crying. Blindly, I took the warm hand touching mine. "It's okay," said the voice. "You're okay." I opened my eyes, and Jordan was kneeling beside me, holding my hand in his. "It's okay . . . It's going to be okay."

It had started to rain, and Jordan led me down the hill to my bike. He let go of my hand in order to pull the bike upright and walk it across the grass, heading in the opposite direction from my house.

"I'm taking you to my house because my mom would kill me if I left you out in the rain." He smiled, his eyes not leaving mine. The wet grass slapped against my bare legs, and the rain that filled the air with a dusky perfume also trickled down my hair in little rivers.

Jordan's house looked snug, tucked behind a stand of old maples. Through the trees I could just make out the graveyard on the hill, and I suddenly realized I was going to a stranger's house. I mean, I didn't know Jordan at all. Maybe he was an axe murderer or something and had a dozen bodies hidden in the basement. I looked at him, walking my bike through the rain, his hair soggy from standing outside holding my hand. I wondered why he would care about me, but for some reason, he seemed to. He propped my bike against the massive maple next to the driveway. Flowers fringed the stones, all different colors—daisies, pansies, tea roses, and others I didn't know. The smell from the flowers and the wet soil made me want to lie down on a big pile of leaves and sleep.

A woman opened the door, and held it open for us. Her dark hair hung in tight ringlets to her shoulders, and she had kind eyes. She reminded me of Megan's mom, with her apple cheeks, only her skin was darker.

"Jordan, who is this?"

"Mom, this is Julie. Julie, this is my mom, Celeste."

She took my hands, held them in hers, and looked into my eyes. "Julie, nice to meet you. Come on in and get warmed up. Your hands are ice cold! Jordan, go get her a towel."

Jordan went off to find a towel, and Celeste led me into the living room. I met Jordan's sister, Sheree, and her son, Trevor. I'm not great at guessing babies' ages, but I think he looked about ten or eleven months old. He was plopped on a colorful mat (you know the kind, with mirrors and squeaky things and painted-on bullseyes) like a big sweet potato. He smiled at me, showing his one gleaming white tooth and a shining gob of drool on his chin. Jordan's sister sat with him, shaking a rattle. She looked up at me and nodded hello, and I thought that she looked extremely tired.

The smell of roasting meat filled my nostrils when Celeste said, "Now, Julie, you are welcome to stay for dinner—we have plenty."

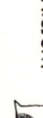

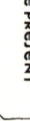

I know this sounds weird, but dinner at Jordan's house was difficult because they were so nice—even to each other, you know what I mean? It was like I was starving, and they had this feast set out that they had every day—feasting on ham and turkey and fresh apple pie, while I'm sitting here chewing on an old bone. I mean, they had what my life could've been like if my parents weren't acting like such you-know-whats. It made me so sad.

After dinner, Jordan's dad Gerald put my bike into their van. I sat in the front seat, with Jordan in the back, and he drove me home. I don't know what we talked about though, because I suddenly remembered that I had forgotten to tell Mom I wouldn't be home for dinner, and I had completely forgotten about Rudy. We pulled up outside the house, which was dark even though Mom's car was there. Jordan's dad left the engine running while Jordan hauled out my bike and put it in the garage. He closed the garage door and took a piece of paper out of his pocket.

"Give me a call, if you want," he said.

I looked down at the paper: *Jordan Vincent*. It had his phone number.

"Thanks, Jordan, for everything," I said and hugged him kind of awkwardly, feeling like

I had an extra arm or something. I waved from the porch as they drove away, and then turned toward the door. I had my hand on the knob when it opened in my hand and revealed Mom and Rudy. Rudy came squiggling out, his rear end wagging so much I thought it was going to disconnect itself and fly off like a rocket. He slurped at my hand, whining as if I'd been gone forever. Mom leaned against the door, staring at me, her eyes glinting in the lamplight.

"I'm sorry, Mom, I completely forgot to call, but it is okay because my friend Jordan took me to his house for dinner." I spoke quickly to try to head off whatever storm was coming. She held up her hand, like, stop-talking-or-else, and I stopped talking.

"I come home," she said quietly, "and the dog is alone, hungry, and needing to go out. I find no note, no message . . . nothing." Her lips tightened into a thin line, and I squinted my eyes and braced myself for the enormous wave that was about to hit. But all she said was, "Julie, come in. You're shivering."

Mom had fed Rudy and let him out, I guess, because there were no messes or anything. There was lasagna out on the table and some salad.

I looked at Mom as she slowly scratched Rudy's head, watching me eat.

"I'm sorry, Mom," I said, and she nodded.

Later we both got into pajamas, and Mom made a big bowl of popcorn for us to eat as we watched funny videos on television of people doing stupid stuff. One guy tried to ride down this little plywood ramp on a mountain bike and looped right back around, plopping on his head. Another guy was chasing a goose that ended up biting him you-know-where. Mom and I laughed so hard that we knocked the popcorn over, and Rudy immediately pounced on it. He inhaled it without even chewing, I swear, and then he sucked up the crumbs like a vacuum cleaner.

About half an hour later, he got gas—so bad it would have stripped wallpaper off the wall. Whichever of us smelled it first would yell, "Take cover!" and we'd both put our pajama sleeves over our noses and breathe through them like we were sucking back the last oxygen on the planet. I think I said something dumb like, "Gee, Rudy really loves your popcorn, Mom. What'd you put in it, stinkweed?" She whacked me with a pillow, I whacked her back, and Rudy got up, dancing around and gassy. I swear I hadn't laughed so hard in ages.

CHAPTER ELEVEN

I got up earlier than Mom the next day so that I could make her pancakes. I used the recipe she always uses, and I think they turned out pretty well. By the time Mom came out, I had a stack on the table with maple syrup and butter, and I even had hot water for tea.

"Wow!" she said. I could tell she was pleased because she was grinning in this kind of goofy but nice way, and her eyes actually twinkled. I couldn't remember her looking like that for a long, long time, at least not since Dad left. We both plowed into the pancakes, but I got up and down a lot, getting milk, syrup, and more butter. I wanted Mom to feel special, you know?

Rudy's digestion problems had not improved (and it was kind of disgusting trying to eat— I actually gagged), so I put him outside where he yipped and scratched miserably outside the sliding glass doors. I closed the blind and put on nice music, and we could hardly hear him after that.

Mom and I clinked glasses of milk. "To Rudy," I said.

"To Rudy," said my mom.

After Mom went to work, I went out and threw a ball for Rudy, hoping that some running around would help Rudy work out his digestion issues. When the phone rang in the kitchen, Rudy snapped at my feet as I ran to get it. It was Dad, and you know, for a second I thought about pulling a Megan and hanging up on him, but I didn't.

"Hi, baby," he said, but I didn't say anything.

"Look, babe, I think you and I should go and see someone who helps kids with their problems."

"Why? I'm not the one with the problem."

"We've been over this, Julie. Just stop pretending because it's not helping. Now, I haven't talked to your mother about this—this is between you and me, okay? Look, I'm trying to be the good guy here."

"You're trying, Dad, but you're not listening because you don't listen to anyone—not to Mom and not to me." Rudy stared at me, his brown eyes filled with worry. He's a very sensitive dog, you know.

"So you expect me to believe that Evie would smash her own stuff? I mean, come on, Julie, why would she do that?"

"I've been thinking about that," I said. "Maybe she did it to get me out of your life. It certainly worked, didn't it? You believed her instead of me. Does she even know you're still calling me?" When he didn't answer, I knew she didn't. "You know what, Dad? You walked out on Mom because of Evie. You bailed on our *family* because of her. You know what I think? I think you made a really, really stupid mistake and that *you know it*. But don't worry, because Mom and I are doing fine without you!" I slammed down the phone.

How is it possible that the guy I once thought of as a hero could suddenly seem so small and puny to me? I mean, I remember going shopping with him when I was little and walking in the parking lot. I held on to his finger, and my hand was so small that his one finger was as big as my whole hand. Was this what growing up was? Do you suddenly realize that your parents didn't know what they were doing, either? I went back outside and sat on the step. Rudy tucked himself under my arm, with his head on my lap. I don't know how long we sat there. The air was still, and the sun burned through the thick clouds until they broke off into shapes. One cloud morphed into a dolphin and swam away, and another became a ship and sailed across the sky.

Rudy and I had just eaten lunch when there was a knock at the door. I looked through the peephole and almost fainted with shock—Megan! She was sweaty because she'd ridden her bike over, and for once her hair didn't look so great as it stuck to her head. I opened the door slowly, not sure how to act. I didn't say anything, but Rudy pushed past my leg and put his head under Megan's hand. She kind of stared at this dog—the one who'd thrown up on her—but then she started scratching his head mechanically, and Rudy groaned and leaned against her leg, and that was it. Megan and I started laughing. Rudy has that effect on people.

I held the door open, and Megan came inside with Rudy close behind. She sat on the couch, and I flopped into an armchair as Rudy settled himself across her lap, his eyes closed to sleepy half-moons in a second.

"How've you been?" asked Megan.

"Umm, kind of the same. Some things are better, but some things are way worse."

She nodded, and we didn't say anything for a minute. "Kevin and I broke up," she said, finally. "I broke up with him."

I could hardly believe my ears. "How come? I mean, I thought you were crazy about each other."

She sighed and stroked Rudy's ear. "I don't know. I didn't like myself around him, and then what you said." She looked at me. "I want us to be friends again, Jules. I miss you." It's amazing how things change so fast—like one minute I'm thinking Megan and I will never be friends again, and the next minute we're best friends again. Sometimes life is confusing, but it's okay, you know?

I threw Rudy's tennis ball at her (I know, really mature), and it caught her on the arm and bounced off Rudy's head. He sat up, confused.

"Dodgeball!" I shouted.

"Oh, no you don't," shrieked Megan. She pushed Rudy off her lap and dived after the ball, which had landed between the couch and cushions. When she lobbed it back at me, it grazed Mom's lamp, which wavered between falling and standing upright. I leaped over and steadied it, and Megan gazed heavenward with an I-have-seen-my-death-and-lived expression. I snatched the ball and headed for the sliding glass doors, where Rudy (of course) got jammed with me, and then I ran shrieking to the other end of the backyard with Rudy nipping at my heels.

When Megan followed, laughing, we threw the ball back and forth, playing keep-the-ball-away-from-the-big-stupid-dog until Rudy had flecks of disgusting foam flying off his face. By the time we plopped down in the grass, breathing hard, Rudy was panting like he had just run a marathon or something.

"Geez, Rudy," I said. "Do you need me to call an ambulance or something?" He leaned over and gave me a big, slurping kiss right on the mouth. "Ugh!" I spat in the grass and wiped my mouth on my hand, and Megan cracked up, holding her stomach and lying back in the grass, tears of laughter streaming down her face. It was so good to be friends with Megan again. I told her she didn't need to break up with Kevin to be friends with me, but she said he was kind of getting on her nerves anyway, so that was okay, and besides, she and her family were going on vacation for the next two weeks. I didn't tell her about meeting Jordan because I didn't want to start giggling about him, like we always did about boys in school. I wasn't sure how I felt about him. I mean, I was pretty much a mess every time he saw me, but he still liked me. I couldn't figure him out, you know? He probably just liked me as a friend anyway, so it didn't matter.

It was almost dinnertime when Megan left. Rudy and I sat on the front step waving (me, anyway) as she rode away. When she turned to wave back, she veered toward a pole. I screamed, pointing, and she managed to swerve away at the last second. "Can you please try to not kill yourself?" I shouted as she disappeared around the corner. We were still sitting on the step when Mom drove up, and I could tell before she even got out of the car that she'd had a bad day. She slammed the door and walked quickly up the front path.

"Hi, Mom," I said, and Rudy whined. It was almost as if he knew what was coming. I guess I did, too, but I didn't want to know.

Mom glared at me. "I got a phone call from your father today. It seems there was a problem at his girlfriend's house last weekend." The way she said "girlfriend's house," she could have been saying "nest of vipers," and it would have been the same.

"Oh?" I said, my stomach tightening.

Rudy kept whining softly, and Mom glanced down at him irritably and then back at me. "Was there a problem, Julie?" I nodded, my cheeks feeling hot because I felt guilty, even though I hadn't done anything. "Were you ever going to tell me about this?" she asked.

"I . . . I thought I could handle it," I said.

"Julie, I'm your mother. I want to know if something is bothering you."

"But I didn't do it!" I said. "I tried to tell that to Dad, but he won't listen. You believe me, don't you?"

Mom didn't answer for a second. "I don't know what to think," she said. "But, if you didn't do it, why did you hide this from me?"

"I didn't want you to get mad at Dad," I said, but that wasn't all. I also felt kind of dirty, as if somehow I'd been part of something disgusting. I didn't say that part; I don't know why.

Mom glared at me. "Maybe your dad deserves what he gets," she snapped. "All I've ever done is try to . . ." She stopped, closed her eyes, and took a deep breath. "It doesn't matter. So, what's for dinner?" I just kind of sat there with my mouth hanging open. It had been my turn to make dinner, and I had completely forgotten. My mom's eyes literally bulged out of her head. "Julie! You forgot? I asked you to do one simple thing today and you *forgot*?"

"I'm sorry. I'll go right now . . ."

"NO!" said Mom. She opened the door and stomped into the house. "You stay here on the step, sitting comfortably, and I will go and make us both some dinner, even though I've been working *all day!*" Even in the house I could hear her.

"Mom, I said I'll . . ."

"Too late! If you'd wanted to help me, you should've done it *before* I got home. What did you do all day, watch TV? You couldn't fit dinner into your busy schedule?" I heard cupboards slamming.

I sank back down on the step, close to tears. I tried so hard, but so often it seemed like I could never please my mom, and I felt as if all I did was screw up. Finally I got up, threw open the front door, and marched into the living room. Mom was glaring at me from the kitchen, where she had just opened a can of tomatoes.

"Mom!"

She put up her hand to shut me up. "Don't you even start, miss," she said, her eyes narrowing. "I am still your mother, and don't you forget it!"

"I forget to make dinner, and that makes me a terrible person?"

Mom turned back to the stove and dumped the tomatoes into a pan.

"You're not being fair," I said with Rudy by my side, quivering. "All *I* did was forget to make dinner, but *you're* . . ."

Mom came around the kitchen counter and walked toward me, her finger pointed, and her eyes boring holes in me. "Get to your room."

"No! Why should I?"

"GET TO YOUR ROOM," she bellowed and grabbed my arm. I tried to yank it out of her grasp.

There's a blur, a flash of brown as the dog lunges at her. Jaws wrap around her thin arm, and I see the teeth—long and yellow. I marvel at how long they are, but they scare me with their wildness, too. I try to scream—NO, NO, NO—but no words come out as blood blossoms on her shirt sleeve.

CHAPTER TWELVE

I could hear him crying, howling in the garage like a lost child calling for its mother. I put the pillow over my ears, but I could still hear him crying for me. He had only been trying to protect me.

Mom had stared at her bloody shirt, her eyes wide, and then slowly pulled the sleeve up. One puncture mark—it wasn't much, but it was enough.

"He bit me," she said, as if she just couldn't believe it. He hadn't fought it when she had hauled him off by his collar out to the garage, but now his cries were shattering me like glass.

Some time in the middle of the night I left the house. Mom's light was still on in her room, but I made no noise. Even Rudy had stopped howling, as if he could sense I was coming.

I looked through the window. The moon was half-full, coating everything in silver shadow, and stars were flung across the darkness like diamonds—still shining, even after everything. I opened the door to the garage, and I could sense where Rudy was without turning on the light. He was shivering, but not from the cold, and I just sat there, holding him.

Usually I'm freaked out about spiders and getting bugs in my hair and stuff like that, but I didn't even think about it as I held on to that dog for the rest of the night. I woke up to the sound of Mom's car pulling out. I was relieved by the thought of her being gone for the whole day—at least we wouldn't fight again. I think I ate breakfast, but I really don't remember. I just remember how I felt, though "numb" doesn't begin describe it, you know?

I went to visit Elizabeth later, and I took Rudy because I couldn't leave him alone in the house. I didn't know what Mom might do if she came home and I wasn't there. I took it slowly on the bike because Rudy didn't seem to have much energy, and I didn't want to push him. It was as if he could still remember last night, you know? The air felt heavy, as though it was pressing against my head, and thick, sticky-looking clouds swarmed overhead, threatening to rain.

The gravestones greeted us—Willard, Isaac, Frances, and Thomas. Rudy didn't hike his leg around any graves, which I knew I should be glad about, but it seemed kind of sad because he wasn't acting normal. At Elizabeth's grave, I sat and patted the ground for Rudy, and he came and stood in front of me, his muzzle almost touching my nose. I looked into his eyes, the color of earth and leaves and cool water.

"Lie down, buddy," I said softly, and he curled up next to me, settled his head on my lap, and closed his eyes as I stroked his ears. Finally, he fell asleep, and for once he didn't drool. The clouds were gathering, and my head felt like it was on too tight or something. I watched the shadows moving across Elizabeth's grave marker.

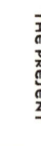

"Elizabeth," I said, "I wonder if you had any problems like these. I mean, I know you were only little when you died, but I bet your mom didn't have problems she couldn't handle and your dad didn't run off." I felt like a whole world of sadness was trying to squeeze out in tears that wouldn't stop, but I swallowed them back down.

I lifted Rudy's head off my lap, settled him on the grass, and walked up and down the hill around Elizabeth's grave, gathering the tiny wild flowers that grew in the grass. I put half of them on her grave and laid the rest on the graves of her parents, John and Emily. Then I sat, looking out over the hill and listening to Rudy snore softly. Seeing the path to Jordan's house through the trees made me think about Jordan, and I realized that I didn't know what to think about Jordan. Part of me hated being around him because I couldn't forget how messed up my life was compared to his, but another part of me loved being around him because he was really easy to talk to, which is unlike any other guy I know, including my dad. It wasn't Jordan's fault that he had the perfect life while mine stank.

I shook Rudy and said, "Come on, buddy—let's go and visit Jordan." We pushed down through the long grass and maples to Jordan's house. There weren't any cars in the driveway, but that didn't mean he wasn't home. I remembered his saying that his mom, Celeste, worked as a nurse, and Gerald worked with computers. Jordan's sister went to college full-time, so that meant he might be home alone with his nephew.

I rang the doorbell, and Jordan opened the door so fast I kind of screamed.

He laughed. "Sorry, Julie. I just put Trevor down for a nap, and I didn't want the doorbell to wake him up." He opened the door wide so I could get past. "What's up?"

"Oh, nothing," I said. "Just checking in with Elizabeth."

"Yeah? What is it with you and that kid?" he asked. He said it with a smile on his face, but it seemed like he thought I was some kind of freak, which hurt my feelings a little, you know? I just shrugged. Rudy had made himself at home, stretching out in the middle of Jordan's living room like he had lived there his whole life. I said something about needing to fetch his slippers and make him a snack, and Jordan laughed.

"So, what's up?" he asked again.

"Nothing. I just wanted to say hi," I said. "What's up with you?"

"Nothing," he said. "I get to look after my baby nephew all summer instead of going out with my friends." He flopped on the couch. "And you?"

I slouched in the armchair and didn't say anything.

"It's that bad, huh?"

"Last night Rudy bit my mom."

Jordan bolted upright, blinking like he had heard it wrong, but I just frowned and nodded. "Mom and I were fighting, and he was trying to protect me."

"What'd you do?"

"I didn't do anything; I just stood there, watching Rudy jump at her. He broke her skin."

Jordan shook his head. I swear he must have thought I had the most messed-up family, and I wouldn't have argued.

"And you know what else?" I said. "My dad's girlfriend threw around her stuff and broke it, really expensive stuff, like glass ornaments. Guess who she blamed?"

Jordan didn't say anything.

I went on. "Me—of course she blamed me. Then she kicked me out. I even wrote my dad a letter saying how I didn't do it, but he didn't believe me." I closed my eyes. "I envy you so much."

"Why?"

"Because your life is so great, and your mom and dad are so cool. I mean, you guys talk to each other—you even seem to like each other."

Jordan didn't say anything for a second. "Julie," he said, and I opened my eyes. He was staring at me with a funny expression on his face. "My life isn't so easy, either."

"Jordan, you don't even know how lucky you are. You have this perfect life, where people care about you and wonder where you are if you come home too late."

Jordan stood up, looking upset, and I knew I'd said something wrong, but I wasn't sure what. My head felt like it was being squeezed, and I suddenly wished I hadn't come over.

"You know, Julie," he shook his head, licking his lips as if he'd tasted something bad. "You know, you come in here and look around for a minute, and you decide I've got it made. Yeah, my family is great most of the time, but they aren't perfect, either. I wasn't asked if I wanted to stay home and take care of my sister's baby for the summer, I was *told* I was going to do it. I know she doesn't have the money to pay someone else, but still . . ."

His eyes softened and he knelt in front of me, putting his hand on the arm of the chair. "Julie, if your life is messed up, fix it. You have to fix your own life." He took my hand, but then looked shocked when I yanked it back.

"I really thought you'd understand," I said, shaking my head and biting my lip to keep from crying.

"Julie, I wasn't trying to be mean, I was just saying." He reached for my hand again. *The ocean hammers against my skull, but there's no safe place and nowhere to go.* I pushed his hand away and scrabbled my way out of the armchair.

"It was stupid of me to come over," I said, heading for the door with Rudy beside me. Jordan looked like he was going to try to convince me to stay, but Trevor started to cry from the bedroom.

I pedaled, one foot and then the other, with Rudy running beside me—always beside me. The phone was ringing when I got home, but I ignored it and fed Rudy instead. Then I shut the blinds to the afternoon light and fell into bed.

Ink fills my eyes and my nose, and I breathe black liquid into my lungs, causing them to burn. I turn around and around, swimming, struggling, and scraping my hands through liquid so thick it congeals around me. I can't see. I can't see which way to swim.

CHAPTER THIRTEEN

Rudy was nervously licking my face when I woke up. He gets upset when I dream because I must cry or whatever and scare him. Anyway, I woke up with dog slobber all over my face, so I got up to wash it off. When I opened my door, Mom was standing right outside, like she'd been waiting for me. Her clothes were wrinkled, her hair uncombed, and she had a bandage where Rudy had bitten her that covered a purple bruise with yellow edges.

"Have you found a home for that dog yet?" She put a hand heavily on my shoulder, but I shrugged it off.

"Why?"

Her eyes widened, and she leaned into me. "Why? Because he bit me!" She lifted her arm and pointed at the bandage, frowning.

"He was protecting me," I retorted. Her nostrils flared, her eyes narrowed, and she turned and walked out of the house.

I scrambled a couple of eggs and ate on the back step, and Rudy, who hadn't eaten yet, plopped down in front of me, wearing his you-never-feed-me look. I threw him half an egg and thought about what Jordan had said. It really hurt my feelings, but I couldn't really figure out why except that maybe it was because I thought he had it so good. However, maybe he was in a situation he hated, too, and was just acting brave about it, you know? So what did that make me? He had told me that I needed to fix my own life. It upset me at the time because I guess I had just expected him to be my shoulder to cry on, but he was right. The trouble was, I didn't know what to do to fix it.

I got the phone and realized I didn't have Jordan's number on me, so I went through the dirty clothes on my bedroom floor until I found the pants I had been wearing the night he dropped me off. His phone number was still in the pocket.

When he answered, I opened my mouth to talk, but nothing came out. "Hello? Hello?" he said. I hung up, and Rudy stared at me like I was an idiot, so I pushed him away with my foot, but he came back and sat next to me, still staring.

"Now what?" I asked. His brown eyes were unblinking.

I redialed Jordan's number, and he picked it up and said "Hello!" in a please-stop-bugging-me kind of voice.

"Hi," I said.

"Julie?"

"Yeah."

"Julie, I'm sorry I . . ."

"No." That's all I said—just no. I took a deep breath, and I could feel the ocean about to surge in my head, but I said no to that, too. Then I said, "Jordan, don't you dare be sorry because, well, you were right about everything."

Rudy sighed and sank to the ground, covering my feet with his soft fur as he closed his eyes and smacked his lips.

"I just . . ." I paused. "I just don't know how to *fix* it, you know?"

"You'll figure it out," he said.

I nodded, and then realized he couldn't see that, so I said, "Yeah."

"Hey, are you going to be visiting Elizabeth any time soon?"

"I guess so."

"Call me when you go. I'll come with you."

"Thanks."

"Trevor the Terror is awake so I've got to go, but call me, okay?"

"Okay. Bye." I scratched Rudy's ears because he's a smart dog.

I fed Rudy and threw a ball for him for a while. I needed time to think about everything, especially what I was going to do. I worked with Rudy on some tricks. He had forgotten the "Bang" one, so we practiced that until he was flopped on his back again, impersonating road kill. He knew how to shake hands, come, and stay.

"Hey, we should go visit Evie again—destroy another of her desserts!" I was joking, but it wasn't such a bad idea. Only I'd leave Rudy at home.

I called Dad's number. "Dad, it's Julie."

"Oh, you know, now isn't a good time, babe. Can I call—"

"No, you can't call me back. You're going to come and get me and take me to Evie's house."

"Now I told you that Evie said . . ."

"Put Evie on the phone."

Dad covered the phone, and I heard him talking and then Evie's voice, which sounded angry, but I couldn't make out what she was saying.

She got on the phone. "What do *you* want?"

"I'll tell you, Evie. I'm going to come over there, and you, me and my dad are going to talk."

She laughed. "I don't think so, after what you . . ."

"Fine. I'll call the child protection services. See what they have to say about it." Evie didn't say anything, but I could hear her cat breath going in and out.

"Tell my dad to come and get me within the next fifteen minutes," I said, "or I'm calling right now."

"Now, Julie, honey, calm down . . ."

"*Don't tell me what to do!* I'm hanging up and calling now . . ."

"NO!" she yelled but quickly followed with this weird little laugh, like everything was just fine.

Dad must be listening. "Come on over then," she said sweetly.

Dad turned up, tires squealing, and I came out, but there were no tears of joy and running across the lawn in slow motion like before. Instead, I got in the truck and slammed the door. Dad took off so fast I smelled burning rubber. Oh well, he could get new tires for all I cared. He took the corners so fast we were nearly two-wheeling, and I just hung on and enjoyed the view.

He lurched to a stop in front of Evie's Little House of Tortures, got out, slammed the door behind him, and strode up the driveway. I noticed his hair had more gray in it than before—unmarried life didn't agree with him, I guess. The pines towering over Evie's house filled the air with a clean, honest smell that didn't go at all with the woman living under them but smelled good anyway.

Dad closed the door behind him, not waiting for me, and I thought, *How immature could two adults get?* I wondered if maybe they thought I would go away because I was too afraid to open the door. I admit, my heart was hammering a little, but I opened it anyway. Evie was sitting on the couch, and Dad was at the dining room table, his head in his hands.

"Well?" said Evie.

"Gee, you guys. No *Hi, Julie, how are you?* No *Please sit down?*"

Dad banged the table with his fist, without looking up.

"Say what you want to say to me and get out," said Evie, her green eyes glinting.

"Actually, Evie, I don't want to say anything to you." I walked over to my dad. "I'm here to talk to you, Dad." He said nothing. "You know what really happened, don't you? You know that I was telling the truth the whole time."

Dad looked up at me. "We've been over this, Julie . . ."

"Ask her why she let me come over," I said.

His back stiffened. "There's no need, I know what . . ."

"Honey, don't listen . . ." Evie started in.

"Ask her."

Dad looked toward Evie, not even moving his head, just his eyes. For a second, he didn't say anything. I was holding my breath because this was it; this was everything.

He said slowly, "Why *did* you let . . . ?"

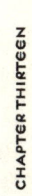

Evie gasped as if she'd never been so insulted in all her life. "You're asking me? You don't believe me now?" She got up from the couch, staring at my dad like a leopard stares at lunch, and practically flung her glass on the coffee table, where it wobbled before falling to the carpet. Her face turned blood red, and I swear I wouldn't have been surprised to see her head shoot off her neck like a bottle rocket. My dad watched her, his mouth hanging open.

She wrenched open the front door and stood ramrod straight beside it. "GET OUT!" she screamed. "GET OUT OF MY HOUSE!"

Dad stood up slowly, shaking his head over and over again like he was trying to wake up from a bad dream.

Evie left her place by the door and flung open the coat cupboard, throwing his coats onto the floor, and kicking at them with her tiny high-heeled feet. "AND TAKE YOUR STUFF WITH YOU!" She attacked his clothes in the bedroom next, dumping them on the cute little puffball shrubs in the front lawn. They looked better out there, anyway.

"Evie," said my dad, holding out his hands toward her. "You lied?"

She froze, goggling at him. Then she laughed. "GET OUT! GET OUT RIGHT NOW!"

CHAPTER FOURTEEN

Fat drops of rain began to spatter the windshield as Dad drove me back home, and he stared silently through it with the empty-eyed shock of an abandoned child. We pulled up to the curb, and he clenched the steering wheel with both hands as he looked at the house. I could tell he wanted to walk in there as badly as I wanted him to. How can things get so messed up?

"Dad?" I touched his hand, taking a deep breath. "Remember how you always promised you'd take me out for a coffee?" He frowned, his eyebrows scrunched, and shook his head no. "Yeah, I know, but you should have, so why not take me now? Please?" Dad grunted, put the truck into gear, and pulled away again. We parked and got out at a coffee shop near the supermarket. I hooked my arm through his and steered him inside.

"I hope you've got some money because I haven't," I said. He looked at me, and for just a second I thought he smiled as he got out his wallet. I ordered for both of us, and we sat at a table near the window, watching people walk by, holding hands or pushing shopping carts. I blew on my hot chocolate, and Dad stared at his coffee. Finally, I added some cream and two packets of sugar—just the way he likes it—and pushed the coffee toward him.

Slowly, he lifted it up and sipped it, smacking his lips a little and nodding. Then he blinked and shook his head like he was still trying to wake up. I looked at him over my cup of hot chocolate: the dark circles under his eyes, gray hair, and sunken cheeks. There was no sparkle in his eyes, either, and it made me sad when I realized his eyes looked just like Mom's.

"Dad," I asked. "Why did you leave?" He put down his coffee and shut his eyes, which caused a tear to slide down his nose and drip onto the table, where it became a tiny puddle.

"I . . . don't know," he said, his voice husky. "I . . ." His voice trailed off, and he shook his head, causing more tears to plop into his coffee.

"Have you ever thought of talking to Mom about it?" I asked. He looked out the window, like he was staring out a million miles away, you know? Maybe he was thinking about some happy times with Mom? There had to be a few, didn't there?

He wiped his face with the back of his hand. "I don't want to talk about it with you, Julie." I kind of blinked at him and gave him my best you've-got-to-be-kidding look. I mean, I know he was hurting, but so was I.

"Why not?" I said. "Your girlfriend accused me of doing all sorts of stuff, and you believed her. Now I'm trying to be mature about it and maybe help you, and *you don't want to talk about it with me?*" My voice got kind of shrill and quivery, which caused people to stare. "How about saying I'm sorry, Julie, for walking out on you. I'm sorry, Julie, for believing that woman over you. I'm sorry . . ."

"That's enough," said my dad, slamming the cup on the table. Hot coffee gushed out the top, scalding his hand, and he put it to his mouth, shaking his head and holding up his other hand to me like a police officer stopping traffic. My face turned bright red, and as we walked out of the coffee shop, I swear I could feel every single person's eyes on my back. We drove back home in silence.

———

I stood in the rain, watching him drive away to who-knows-where, bags full of shirts and underwear flapping in the back of his pick-up truck, and it was weird—even though I felt angry, I also felt sorry for him. I opened the front door and listened. The silence caused me to sigh with relief until I realized Rudy hadn't come out to meet me. I quickly tiptoed inside and shut the door. I looked on the couch, but there was no Rudy. I looked down the hall and noticed Mom's door was closed. If Mom was asleep, then Rudy had to be here somewhere. I mean, he couldn't grab the keys and drive himself to the edge of town.

"Just calm down," I muttered to myself as the hinges on my bedroom door squeaked like a haunted house. I crept up to the bed and patted the bedclothes, in case he was lurking under there, but there was nothing there. I returned to Mom's door and listened to the muffled snort and the sound of blankets rustling coming from inside her room. My heart was doing flip-flops as I stood in the hallway, convinced that something had happened to Rudy. Suddenly, I heard him whine.

"Rudy?" I whispered, and he whined again and scratched at a door. He was trapped in the bathroom right next to Mom's room! He whacked his head when I opened the bathroom door because he came out too fast, but he was too excited to care. His tail was on wagging overdrive, and I swear I almost choked him to death because I hugged him so hard. His eyes kind of bulged, but he managed to lick me pretty much all over my face. I was so happy to see him that I didn't mind at all.

"What were you doing in there, you stupid dog?" I said. "Did you drink toilet water and get trapped? It serves you right, you big dummy!" I buried my face in his fur. "I thought Mom had given you the chop, Rudy."

"You thought Mom had done what?" Mom asked, standing in her doorway. She startled me, so I screamed while Rudy winced. I tried to laugh it off. "Oh, good morning, I mean afternoon. I didn't know—"

"Yes, I'm awake," She said and smiled, but it didn't reach her eyes. "You thought I had done what, Julie?"

For a split second, I felt so afraid, you know? I was kneeling on the floor, holding on to my dog and the only thing in the world that I had. Mom stood over me. She held out her hand toward me, and I gazed at it in confusion until I realized she just wanted me to take her hand. I grabbed it, and she pulled me up.

She didn't let go as she looked into my eyes. "Tell me." I stared down at my feet and noticed the strap on my left sandal was coming loose; I would need to get another pair soon. *"Tell me."*

"I thought you might have put him down," I said slowly.

She let go of my hand. "I wouldn't do that, Julie. You know that."

"You mean he doesn't have to go? Oh, Mom, thank you! I swear he'll never do another bad thing."

"I didn't say that." Her eyes didn't blink, and she continued to stare into mine. "He's going, but I would never put him to sleep without telling you or without letting you say goodbye. I want you to know that." She looked away. "If you can find him another home, that's fine, but they'll have to know he's vicious . . ."

"He is not!" I said. "You know what happened. He thought you were going to hurt me."

She pointed at Rudy, her finger shaking. "That dog is dangerous, and I will not have him in my house."

"It's my house, too," I said. "Rudy is part of this family."

"Not any more," said Mom.

Anger flared up from my throat. "You're right!" I screamed. "Because there is no family."

Mom flinched, but I continued. "You drove Dad away because he could never do anything right, but you know what else, Mom?" My breath came in ragged gasps. "I'm scared of you. If you're such a great mom, then why am I afraid all the time?" She stared at me, saying nothing, with her lips shaking. "You think you're the only one who's going through anything? You and Dad have completely forgotten about me because you only care about yourselves and your own stupid problems. It's pathetic that my dog cares about me more than you do!"

Mom fell back against the wall as if she'd been struck. Her face crumpled slowly and she bowed her head, tears dropping from her face and making dark, wet stains on the rug.

I watch the girl stumble away. I watch from the ceiling, where it is safe. I follow behind as she lurches down the hallway, holding on to her dog's collar, and throws open the front door, stumbling down the front stairs with that dog. They disappear down the street, into the dusk. I see everything, and I worry. I worry about that girl.

CHAPTER FIFTEEN

Car lights swerved in front of me, followed by a horn blaring loudly. Rain spattered my face as I gazed around me, disorienting me so that I wasn't even sure where I was. Houses lined the street with big trees leaning over them. I felt as if I should know this street, but I was so tired that it was like I was looking through fog. Something pulled my hand, and I looked down. I was clutching Rudy's collar so tightly my knuckles glowed white under the street lamps. He pulled again, leading me to the end of the street and a two-story white house with red shutters—Megan's house. There was a car in the driveway and a light on in the living room. I banged on the door, but when nobody answered, I banged again, harder and longer this time.

"Megan!" I shouted, peering through the glass door. There was no movement inside, and the light was only on to keep the burglars away, just like every other summer when they went on vacation. At that point, my legs just kind of gave out, and I sank to the porch. Rudy stood beside me, gently whining and wagging his tail. Suddenly, he stiffened, and I could see the fur on his back stand straight up. He was staring at the road where a car was driving slowly past, the driver's face barely visible, but I could tell that, whoever the guy was, he was staring straight at me. The car went a little further and started to make a slow U-turn.

"Come on, Rudy," I whispered as I jumped off the porch, and we ran for Megan's backyard before the car completed its turn. Rudy and I watched from behind the hedge as it drove slowly past the house again, and Rudy growled deep in his chest. There was a sturdy-looking branch out on the lawn. When the car had passed, I ran out and grabbed it, but not before slipping on the wet grass. I scrambled back behind the hedge, and my heart thundered in my ears. I held the branch like a baseball bat. Rudy's lip was curled up and his teeth bared. If the psycho found us, he'd have way more than he could handle—Rudy and I would make sure of it.

The car drove back and forth a couple more times before finally taking off. I felt all rubbery and shaky, but I couldn't just hide in Megan's backyard all night. I waited another five minutes before we climbed out of the hedge. I was soaked, and I had no idea where I was going or what I was going to do.

We walked back along the same road. I kept a tight hold on the stick, and Rudy and I slipped from bush to bush for a while until we were sure we weren't being followed. Whenever a car came, we hid behind something until it passed. Eventually we came to a long stretch where there were no houses, just some scattered trees and a deep ditch—the same one I'd fallen into what felt like years ago now.

The moon was covered by clouds, and drizzle fell in a hazy curtain. I started shivering because I was soaked and my legs were bare. After a car nearly missed hitting Rudy and me, I thought it was probably safer to walk in the ditch and started down the bank. My stupid sandal chose that moment to finally break, and I tripped and slid down, thumping against the other side of the ditch and scratching my leg on the stick.

I just kind of lay there for a second, wishing that it wasn't happening and wanting someone to please wake me up now. Rudy stood over me, his ears dripping, and even in the weak moonlight

I could tell his dark eyes were sad. I dropped the stick and hauled myself up, with only one sandal on, and sloshed through the ditch. Rudy walked in front of me, turning every couple of feet or so to make sure I was still following. When cars passed by, I lay against the bank so they couldn't see me, and Rudy crouched right down, too.

When I finally saw the hill in the distance, I knew where I had been walking to this whole time. I used a clump of weeds for a handhold and crawled out of the ditch. Tall maples surrounded Jordan's house, and they were bathed in warm light that shone from the house's windows. Jordan's family would help me, maybe take me in, let me get cleaned up, and loan me some dry clothes.

I walked up the little path edged with his mom's flowers and stood in front of the door, my hand raised to knock. I could see them in the living room. Jordan was stretched out on the floor, his hands behind his head, watching a movie while Celeste and Gerald sat on the couch, his arm around her shoulder. Sheree was reading a textbook at the kitchen table. It was late, so Trevor was probably in bed. I realized my hand was still poised in mid-air, ready to knock, but I couldn't do it; I couldn't make my problem their problem, you know? When I turned away from the door, Rudy looked at me like he was confused.

"Come on," I said, and he did, even though I knew he wanted to go in there as badly as I did.

We climbed up the hill. It was dark, and the rain was heavier now, creating little rivulets that flowed down my neck and back. There were no streetlights up there, and the moon was hidden by clouds. Around the perimeter of the hill, the trees stood black and motionless. My foot slipped out of my broken sandal, and I fell hard on my knee. I patted the ground until I found the shoe, but only so I could fling it down the hill. I was better off without it.

We kept walking. The hill seemed bigger in the dark, and the only sounds were of the rain spattering against the grass and Rudy's and my breathing. The lights of the cars below seemed like glowing, snaking worms, but they had no real relation to us. We were outside of the world, outside of time. The gravestones appeared out of the dark, jutting like broken teeth, and Rudy started to whine. I ignored him and threaded my way through the stones. Willard, Isaac, Frances, and Thomas—I couldn't read their names in the dark, but I knew they were there.

"Hello," I said when I reached Elizabeth. I sat next to her grave, hugging my knees for warmth and comfort as rain dripped off my hair and into my eyes. I could just make out the outline of her gravestone and thought about how she was just two years old—that's all—and then she was gone. Rudy sat in front of me, whining. He wouldn't stop whining.

"Stop it," I said. Maybe he didn't understand me, because he kept doing it. "Stop whining!" I was very clear, but he wouldn't stop. I breathed in slowly, trying to fight the feeling welling inside, but I really wanted to make him stop, you know? I just wanted him to shut up. I breathed slowly and turned my attention back to the grave. "Elizabeth, I feel like you're my sister. I know it sounds stupid, but I feel like I know you somehow. You had the right to live and have a happy life, but you didn't have that."

Rudy hadn't stopped whining the whole time, and I suddenly just lost it. "RUDY!" I screamed, and he cringed and backed away from me, which just made me angrier for some reason. "RUDY, JUST SHUT UP OR . . . OR I'LL . . . I'LL . . ."

I started to sob—great heaving sobs that felt like my whole insides were going to come out. I tore at the grass with my hands and pounded the dirt. Rudy came toward me, still whining. I swung my arm and hit him, catching him behind the ear and knocking him to the ground. He yelped, scrambled to his feet, and ran a few steps away. Then he just stood there, whimpering louder.

"SHUT UP!" I screamed and ran at him with my hands balled up until he turned and ran into the dark, whimpering and with his tail tucked. I stood breathing hard, my hands curled into hard fists. After a while, my breathing slowed, and I was alone. It seemed as if everything in my life had led me to this moment. I was alone, shivering, but unable to care about any of it. I knelt on Elizabeth's grave, staring at the stone that glowed pale like a fading beacon in the dark. I lay over the grave, face up, eyes open, and arms outstretched. Rain rushed toward me, and I closed my eyes and opened my mouth to receive it. I was finished trying to fix what was broken. The ocean washed over me, surging over the walls.

I watch from above and see the girl who is lying on the child's grave. She looks cold and pale, and my tears shower from the sky, streaming down my own cold cheeks, for the girl. I realize with a shock that I love her and that I don't want to leave her alone any more. I reach down to hold her and gather her in my arms, and I feel the rain on my face, my legs, and my outstretched arms. The earth feels soft beneath me. Perfume from the soil fills my nostrils . . . the smell of rain on earth. I breathe deep and hold on as the world spins.

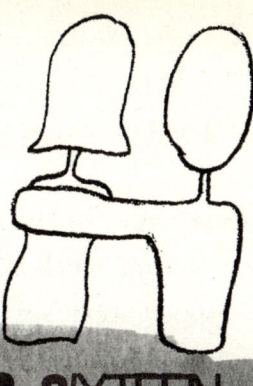

CHAPTER SIXTEEN

I lay in the rain a long time until I finally noticed I was alone. I sat up, looking around for Rudy, and then I got to my feet as soon as I remembered.

"Rudy!" I called, running among the gravestones. "Rudy!" I strained to see into the thick darkness. "Rudy, please come!" The rain fell so heavily I could hardly see a foot in front of me. I ran, traversing the hill, my bare feet sliding on the wet grass. "Rudy!"

I had hit him, but what was worse was that, for a split second, I had *hated* him. Somehow he had known, had felt it, and now my Rudy was gone because I had driven him away. I ran, yelling his name, covered in mud and wet grass, with wet hair clinging to my face. Finally, at the far end of the hill, on the side furthest away from the graveyard, I found him. I couldn't see him, and he didn't make a sound, but I knew he was there.

He didn't move as I walked steadily through the tall grass toward him, but I knew he was watching me. I stopped about six feet away and crouched down. "Rudy," I called softly, apologetically. "Rudy."

He was hiding under a tall shrub, almost completely blended into the deep shadow. I knelt and crawled on my hands and knees under the bush with him. I didn't say anything; I just pressed my face against his and stroked his damp fur. I lay down under the branches and opened my arms, and he didn't even hesitate before crawling into them. I held him, rocking him back and forth the way you do with a baby. "I love you," I said, over and over. "I love you, and I am so sorry."

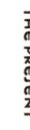

The rain stopped in the middle of the night as we slept under the shrub, holding on to each other. When I woke up, sunshine glinted off the drops of water, glimmering on the branches above us. With my head resting on Rudy's back, I looked up through the branches and into the bluest sky I had ever seen. My clothes stuck to me as I crawled out from under the bush. Rudy was still lying down, his legs poking out sideway like four hairy sticks. When he got to his feet, he bumped his head against the branches, and a cascade of drips fell on him. I laughed and hardly even recognized the sound I was making, you know? I didn't know what would happen or what I was going to do, but I thought that maybe things were going to be okay now. So I laughed some more.

Rudy barked at me, grinning. He was happy, too. I turned and ran across the open grass, with Rudy beside me, until I slipped and fell on my backside. It didn't hurt until Rudy jumped on top of me. He sat there, grinning and panting, as a gob of his slobber fell down on my chin. It was so gross that I couldn't help but laugh, which then caused Rudy to start licking my face.

"You're a good dog, Rudy," I said and scratched behind his ears, even though they were covered with mud. There were a few wormy apple trees on the hill that must have been part of an old orchard, and Rudy chomped on a few fallen apples, chewing them sideway as if he couldn't quite figure out how to eat them. One less-wormy apple was within my reach on one of the lower branches. It was still hard, but I bit into it anyway and spat it out again.

"Ugh! That is so—" but my train of thought was interrupted when I spied a familiar car was parked on the roadside down the hill. Mom.

For a second, I really didn't know what to do. The ocean lurched in my head while I just stood and breathed. Part of me wanted to run but another part of me thought that she wouldn't be here if she didn't, well, care, you know? I couldn't tell if she was in the car, and I couldn't see her on the slope. I turned to look toward the graveyard and there she was, walking between the graves, her head turning from side to side as if she was searching for something. Then she stopped and looked across the meadow as if she could feel me looking at her. She started to run toward me, then stopped, and then started running again.

A cry welled up from inside me. "Mom!" I ran to her, my feet flying across the earth, and we hugged each other, holding on tight.

"Julie," she said. "Julie." I squeezed my eyes shut, feeling her arms around me, knowing it was okay, really okay. Rudy stood to one side with this forlorn look on his face.

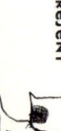

"Rudy," Mom called to him. She let go of me and knelt in the grass, her arms wide. "Come here, boy." Rudy waggled over to her, his rear end threatening to fall off from wagging so hard, and he licked her face and chin. "Yes, you are a good boy," she said. When she finally stood up, her jeans had wet circles at the knees.

"Mom," I said. "I didn't mean . . ." All of a sudden I couldn't talk because my throat got so tight, you know? All I could do was just look into her soft amber eyes. I couldn't remember really looking in her eyes before.

She laid her hand against my cheek. "Julie, you have nothing to apologize for. Everything you said to me was true, but one thing you need to know is how much I love you. Even when I screw up so badly and behave like . . ." A tear slid down her cheek. "I am so sorry for what I did. I won't ever . . ." Her face screwed up, and she choked out, "I'll never leave you again. I promise." Her eyes were puffy and red as tears streamed down her cheeks, but I swear she'd never looked more beautiful to me. "Please . . . Come home?"

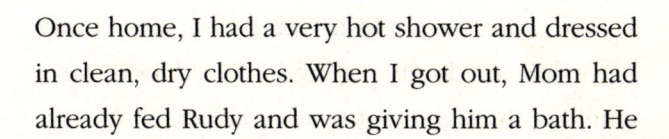

Once home, I had a very hot shower and dressed in clean, dry clothes. When I got out, Mom had already fed Rudy and was giving him a bath. He jumped out and ran around the house, shaking himself and leaving behind a trail of puddles and wet hair. Mom chased him with a towel, calling after him, but she didn't seem to mind too much. As I watched him run by for the millionth time, something occurred to me.

"Mom," I said, "how did you know where to find me?" She slumped into a chair, with Rudy just out of reach, panting and dripping on the carpet. She shook her head and rolled her eyes heavenward.

"I saw your friend Jordan's phone number where you had left it on the table. I called him early this morning and asked if he knew where you might be. He didn't want to say at first, but he finally told me about the little graveyard. He offered to go and look for you, but I wanted to do it." Mom got up and threw the towel at Rudy, who seized it and shook it playfully. "He sounds like a good friend, Julie."

I nodded. "He is."

"Why don't you invite him over for dinner?"

For the rest of that afternoon, Rudy and I played in the backyard and went swimming. I got him to do "Bang" and I could hear Mom laughing through the kitchen window.

That evening, Jordan rode over on his bike, and the three of us sat down to roast chicken, homemade mashed potatoes, broccoli, beans, and a cherry pie for dessert. Mom had been cooking all day, and we had a real feast. You know, I really love her. She's not perfect, but who is? After dinner she said that next time Jordan should bring his whole family over. They sounded like great people, she said, and I said, yeah, they were. Jordan and I helped clear the table and load the dishwasher, and I threw some extra chicken meat into Rudy's bowl because I knew he'd love roast chicken as much as I do.

Mom said Jordan and I could take Rudy for a walk if we wanted because it was such a nice night. So we went out. The stars were really bright, and Jordan pointed out constellations.

"Look, there's Ursa Major. It's the shape of a bear. You see?" he said, pointing. "And Ursa Minor." He connected the dots in the sky for me with his index finger, but to me they still looked like dots.

"How can people see anything but stars?" I said. "I mean, how can you see bears and horses or whatever from just looking at the stars themselves?"

He shrugged. "I like figuring out how they all fit together." He gazed up at the sky with his mouth kind of hanging open, and I swear he looked just like a little kid who'd noticed the stars for the first time. I think that's what I like about Jordan—he's just himself.

"Hey, there's Cassiopeia . . ."

I followed where he was pointing, but I couldn't tell one star from another. Even Rudy stared up at the sky, looking back and forth, like he couldn't figure it out, either. I wondered if he even saw the stars. Anyway, he didn't seem to care one way or another, because he trotted ahead, panting and smiling, waiting for us to follow. We started walking again, with Rudy in the lead, stopping every couple of feet or so to make sure Jordan and I were following.

"Yes, we're right behind you, buddy," I'd say. And then after another two seconds, "Yep, we're still here . . ." Jordan walked Rudy and me back to the house, and we all stood on the porch.

"Do you want a ride home?" I said. "I can go ask my mom?"

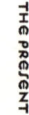

He shook his head. "I'm fine." He tucked a bit of my hair behind my ear and ran his finger along my chin. I swear my heart started beating like there was a jackhammer in there.

He smiled. "I really like you, Julie."

I blushed and couldn't think of anything to say, so I just stood there blushing. Rudy jammed himself between Jordan and me, not wanting to be left out. Jordan leaned toward me and kissed me on my cheek. In my mind I could already hear Megan shrieking and laughing.

After Jordan left, Rudy and I sat on the porch, thinking about everything. Well, I was thinking about everything; Rudy was busy licking himself. I pointed out the constellations to him, and you know, he actually looked up.

"Can you see them, Rudy?" I asked, and as he blinked at the sky, I think he actually saw them for a second.

"They're always there, even when you can't see them. That's what's so amazing."

He looked at me as if I had just blown his mind, so I scratched him behind his ears. "I know, I'm brilliant, aren't I?" Later, as the moonlight played in my room and made the shadows of branches dance across the wall, I lay in bed with my arms around Rudy, who smacked his lips and snored peacefully beside me, and felt so grateful for everything.

I stand at the top of a very high mountain and gaze around me. Mountain ranges roll out before me like waves of a sea. I breathe deeply and smell wildflowers, ice, and stars. I fill my lungs. I look down at the dark, swirling ocean far below. I feel my feet slip, the rock crumbling, giving way, and I fall headfirst into the water's deep, gurgling inky center and feel the cold shock. I remember I have been here before. I hold my breath and swim. For a second, I do not know which way is up, and I swim frantically. My lungs burn. I see a light above me and push through the thick water that carries me upward until I reach the surface. And then I breathe.

EPILOGUE

Elizabeth's grave is in front of me. I touch the smooth stone, running my fingers along its top. Months have passed since I've been here. The daisies I left last time have either disintegrated or blown away. It's cold up here on the hill, and I pull my jacket around me. Jordan sits in the grass, not saying anything, just being with me. The cold doesn't seem to bother him because is coat is unzipped as if it's a spring day. He's always like that. He strokes Rudy's head, which lies curled against his leg. Rudy's winter fur is wiry and thick, making him look even funnier than before, but that's okay.

I crouch in front of Elizabeth's grave marker and sweep off the dead leaves that have fallen around it. Why did I feel so much for this little girl who lived so long before I did? I mean she would have been dead by now, no matter what, you know? I just did. I think maybe it was because things were so bad back in the summer that I felt kind of like I was dead, too, you know? I mean, you know how bad things got.

I'm not sure how I feel about Mom and Dad. Dad's come over for dinner a few times in the last few months, and they act like they want to try again. I mean, they both seem like they've changed. One part of me is really happy about that, I mean really happy, but another part of me is afraid it won't work out and will be like before, or worse. But I believe people really can change, so who knows? I pick up a bright red leaf and place it on her grave. I set a stone on top of it to keep the wind from carrying it away.

"Goodbye, Elizabeth."